HERE'S
Mrs. A

Canada's Woman of the 20th Century

Blessing!
Blessing!!
Ron Pegg

RON PEGG

HERE'S MRS. A.
Copyright © 2014 by Ron Pegg

All rights reserved. Neither this publication nor any part of this publication may be reproduced or transmitted in any form or by any means, electronic or mechanical, including photocopying, recording or any information storage and retrieval system, without permission in writing from the author.

Printed in Canada

ISBN: 978-1-4866-0500-2

Word Alive Press
131 Cordite Road, Winnipeg, MB R3W 1S1
www.wordalivepress.ca

Cataloguing in Publication information may be obtained through Library and Archives Canada.

*Dedicated to
Mrs. A's Grandchildren
And
The Dr. S.R. McKelvey Family*

Acknowledgements

Special thanks to Bert Platt, my friend for over 60 years. Without Bert's continuous inspiration and resources, this book would never have been written. Thanks also to the staff of Flesherton Public Library, who went beyond the call of duty to find some resources.

Prelude

Mrs. A grew up in a home where discipline, hard work, traditional family values, and an abundance of love dominated every happening in her young life. She looked forward every winter to the visit of her Mother's parents, followed by a visit from her Aunt Rebecca, her Father's sister and a visit from Uncle Tom and his wife Fanny. These visits each lasted for close to a month.

In a family of seven with five boys and two girls the young Kate was always treated on the same level as her brothers. The truth is, as an apple of her Father's eye, and with her young feminine ways, she was the recipient of favours that the boys never even dreamed of. Add to this, the future Mrs. A, in spite of what she might indicate, always had a strong will of her own.

Her young life experiences in Beeten were of the utmost importance in molding the "Mrs. A" who became loved across Canada, as well as other places around the world. The key to her radio broadcast's success, according to Mrs. A in an interview after she retired, is that you must be interested in other people. There must be a complete lack of self-interest. You must be able to say, "This is what I saw and this is what I think it means."

Mrs. A travelled 5 times around the world visiting 44 countries, She was the first woman director at the CNE, a fashion expert, a culinary whiz, a business woman, a conservation director for the government, a newspaper columnist, a TV panelist, a club speaker, a champion of the home, and a radio commentator.

Kate covered such events as the wedding of Princess Elizabeth and the Duke of Edinborough, and later the coronation of Elizabeth as Queen, San Francisco's World's Fair, a clam bake in Trinidad, Holy Year in Rome, Cyprus in the Turkish Cypriot Crisis, the Pan- Asiatic Conference, the Hungarian border as refugees, from the October revolution sought to elude Russian guards, President Roosevelt in Washington and Hitler's speech from the Chancellery.

The focus of this book is to relate how the little girl from the home of Robert and Ann Scott in the little rural village of Beeton became the woman rightfully called "Canada's Woman of the 20th Century".

Here's "Mrs. A"
Introduction

At the intersection of Yonge Street and St.Clair in mid-town Toronto one finds the well-known and busy radio station C.F.R.B. One of Canada's best known stations 1010 has been a part of the Canadian landscape for decades. Conveying the "news" has made several of CFRB's personnel well-known and well respected personalities Jack Dennett and Gordon Sinclair are two fine examples. A third was the woman very famous by the nickname "Mrs.A."

Today, 50 miles north of the CFRB studio in a small town cemetery one can find the family plot belonging to the "Aitken" family. If one approaches the large family headstone they can read the inscription Kate Scott Aitken. In the quiet setting it's hard to believe that this is the final resting place of one of Canada's best known people. Many people today still read her cookbooks and probably never give much thought to who this lady was or what became of her. It's a story worth telling.

It was in the summer of 2012 that I met Bert Platt in his office at Tim Horton's in Tottenham. Bert is in the habit of going to Tim's for coffee on most days. He calls it his "office".

Over coffee for Bert, and green tea and a peanut butter cookie for me, I talked about the book "Tribute" which had just been released. I said to Bert that I thought this was the last book about Beeton that I could write.

Bert's immediate response was, "What about Kate Aitken? There has never been a book written devoted to her life." I was momentarily stunned into silence. What Bert, - the Beeton historian, said, had to be true. He would know.

I left that day with my mind whirling with thoughts of Mrs. Aitken. I had grown up in a home where Mother always listened to Mrs. A at noon and following the supper (dinner) meal. I grew up knowing that Mrs. A was very much a part of the Beeton landscape. My only personal contact with her was a story that Mother often repeated. It was Beeton Fall Fair. I was in the baby contest. Mrs. A came to my carriage and said, "What a beautiful baby." As I know of Mrs. A today I do not question that those were her remarks. Similar remarks were made by this gracious lady to each and every baby that she looked at that day, - or any other day.

The big question in my mind was how to get myself inside Mrs. A's character and life to be able to write a book about her. I felt that this would be a long and arduous task. The task began.

To begin with I had purchased, a set of Mrs. A's books "Never a Day So Bright" for the history department in the mid 1960's, through the Banting Memorial School. I still had a couple of the copies of the book. I read it at least a half dozen times. Bert is the son-in-law of Doctor McKelvey who was a close friend of Mrs. A's. Bert had, amongst other articles and books, the Doctor's complete file on Mrs. A, much of which was gathered at the time of the unveiling of the Mrs. A plaque in the Beeton Park in 1973. The Museum on the Boyne in Alliston had a good file. The CNE archives have a complete file on this lady.

In many ways, the most amazing thing was the more I became involved in the facts of this great lady's life, the more amazing became the similarities in her life and in my own.

We were both born in Beeton,- about forty years apart but the Beeton I experienced still possessed, as it still does today, many of the same characteristics. Both Mrs. A and I were born and grew up in a home that also housed our Father's store. Both of our Fathers ran a business on Beeton's Main Street for a quarter of a century. Mrs. A's Mother attended St. Andrew Presbyterian Church in the morning and then went to the Methodist United Church at night. Dad went to the now United Church in the morning and visited both the Anglican and St. Andrews at times later on Sunday.

Here's Mrs. A.

The village events, suppers, the choir, anniversary services, Christmas services, young people's activities were very much a part of Mrs. A's young life at St. Andrews. Similar activities were very much part of my life at Trinity United- my three sisters and I all sang in the choir.

Mrs. A talks of skating on the ice at D.W. Watson's outdoor rink behind the Town Hall. That is the very ice surface where I began my skating.

The excitement of Beeton Fall Fair, the joy of being part of the fair, the community exuberance and concern for local boys at war, and the end of a war live in my memory as they did in Mrs. A's.

Mrs. A moved from Beeton and spent much of her life closer to Toronto, - but she always came back. Everyone knew that her hometown was Beeton. Her daily radio broadcast often had a reminder of this. I t has been said that you can take the girl out of Beeton but you cannot take Beeton out of the girl.

I moved from Beeton forty eight years ago, but as the people of the village know, I keep coming back. I have spoken in churches, to school classes, and even opened the fair. I continue to love helping to raise funds for Beeton centered projects. I have often said that you can take the boy out of Beeton, but you cannot take Beeton out of the boy. I thought this was original until I began studying the life of Kate "Scott" Aiken.

Chapter 1

The Setting

Beeton is found on the eighth concession of Tecumseth Township less than ten miles west of today's highway 400. It was originally called Clarksville but in 1873 it was renamed Beetown because of the village postmaster, D.A. Jones who had developed a keen interest in bees and honey. Mr. Jones travelled to Europe, Asia and to the Holy Land in search of the very best type of bees. Mr. Jones took an exhibit of his Beetown honey to the Crystal Palace Exhibition in London. The honey swept the board. D.A. Jones passed away in 1910 when Mrs. A was almost twenty years of age. He was very much a part of her young life. As the years went by Beetown had become Beeton.

The area around Beeton is excellent farm land. On the farm wheat, oats, corn, barley, turnips, and mangos were grown. Cattle, pigs, chickens, ducks, and horses were all part of the livestock. These farms, in the winter time, have been described by Kate to be like a painting. The farmhouse had smoke curling lazily towards the sky from its brick chimney. There was a well-worn path between the house and the barn. Stacks of golden straw were piled outside the stable where the cows would browse before returning to their stalls. Many of the cows in this lazy farm time were allowed to go dry. Hens grew fat and lazy and the number of eggs that were laid decreased. The most available source of fuel was wood. The farm folk spent much of their shorter winter work days cutting this wood to keep the fires glowing.

Much of the activity of the area was centered in the three village churches. The Anglican and Presbyterian Church were found on the west end of Main Street. The Anglican Church's architecture spoke plainly of its English heritage. The much plainer St. Andrews Presbyterian reflected the everyday Scottish heritage of most of the members, as well as the simplicity and hard work behind the scenes of its namesake, Andrew. This church was built in the very year of Mrs. A's birth 1891. The building was completely debt free on the day it was completed. The Methodist Church was part way down the tree studded Centre Street just beyond the business section. It was from this present day United Church that great gospel singing could be heard mixed with the many "Amens".

Saturday was the day that most of the farm folk came to town. The streets were crowded with horse-drawn sleighs in the winter and buggies in the summer. Weekdays in the winter saw the farmers come to town with their grain to be milled into food for their farm animals. The village kids loved to hitch their own sleighs to the farmers sleighs and get a ride to the edge of the village and then catch another sleigh for a ride back into the centre of town.

Chapter 2
Family Roots

To have a stocky Irish Father and a slender gracious Mother with a Scottish background was truly Canadian in the 19th century. Kate's Father; Robert Scott, was one of a family of ten. In 1846 the family had left Ireland because of the disastrous potato famine. They settled in the area of Guelph. Robert's mother died when he was very young. His eldest sister, Rebecca, became the main person in charge of raising this young brood of ten.

Ann Kennedy Scott, Kate's mother, was born on a homestead farm just outside of Guelph, Ontario. Ann's mother had come to Canada with her grandparents from Edinburgh Scotland. The Grandparents had been part of the printing business in Scotland. They opened a book store in Guelph. It was here that Kate's grandmother would meet a dashing young man who had just come from the United States. They were married when she was only seventeen. They entered the pioneer life of developing a homestead. It was a few years later that their daughter Ann came into the Country Cross Roads grocery store to trade eggs and butter for tea, sugar, and spices. The store's clerk was a young Irish man; it was love at first sight. The eighteen year old Ann was not so sure, but after a year of courting the two were married on a cold blustery day at the end of January.

They left Guelph to come to Beeton. The trip included a train ride to Toronto, Ann's first night in the big city, and a second train trip from

Toronto to Bradford. The trip from Bradford to Beeton was on a sleigh. They were kept warm with blankets and their heavy coats. Warmed bricks were at their feet.

Robert and Ann would have seven children. There were five boys and two girls. The children showed the maturity of their upbringing as each followed careers which suited each personality. One brother, Frank, became a doctor, Earl a policeman, Jack a dentist, Bruce became a prosperous insurance and real estate agent, and Walter's field was working as a drug company executive. Kate's baby sister, Margaret, became a nurse. There was no question that Robert and Ann had a home where discipline was very important. Each child was taught the value of work. Each child found it necessary to be competitive with each of their siblings because each one was a strong human being. Their parents encouraged each child to develop the individuality that was in them.

Chapter 3

Robert Scott

Robert's mother died when he was very young. The family of ten was raised by their fourteen year old sister, Rebecca. Rebecca believed the old-country idea that one boy should go into the ministry, one boy should stay on the farm, and a third son should be in the military. Robert was sent to Rockwood Military Academy. He loved it. He became a captain in the Queen's Own Regiment. However, at twenty-eight years of age, he left the regiment in order to buy a country grocery store. Robert had dreams and desires that could not be fulfilled in an everyday military life, although he still had a love for the military. When he arrived in Beeton, Robert used the third floor of the original store to drill the local reserves, as he still was a reserve officer.

He and his wife went to military balls that were hosted in Cookstown. Robert loved to get into his dress uniform with the scarlet coat, the navy blue pants, and the dress sword to attend the ball. In truth, anytime there was a reason to dress up, Robert would be sure to be in military uniform.

When a recruiting campaign came to the Beeton area for the Boer War at the turn of the century, Robert had the urge to enlist. Ann reminded him that he had a family of seven and a business. The urge passed. The military training that had been a major part of his life would always be a part of him. It was an important factor in the discipline of the family.

The personality that found the everyday military life too confining made for a fascinating man. On any given day Robert would be singing. He could be easy going and the next day he would become very strict with his family. On Sunday mornings, he often was up singing gospel songs, as he played the organ in the family parlour. The children loved to hear his beautiful music. Both Robert and Ann sang in the choir at St. Andrews. It was a regular happening to have the choir hold its final practice before the special Christmas service in the Scott home. The practice was part of the choir's Christmas party.

Robert loved to have other people around. Ann always had to have food prepared for many more people than their family. The help in the store ate with the Scotts. Customers who came to shop around noon time were often invited to eat at the Scott table. The store would be closed when the town bell rang at noon. It was the signal for everyone to sit down and eat. Besides customers and the help, a salesman who happened to be in town, visitors to the village who had come to the Scott store, relatives who were in town, boarders in the Scott home, and neighborhood friends could all be part of a meal.

The children loved this open house because their lives were always packed with excitement. On Sunday evenings, the children gathered around their Father as he dramatically read some of the great Bible stories. The children would feel that they were actually at the scene of the event when the walls of Jericho came crashing down or when David killed the lion.

Robert was very popular in the village. He became the Reeve of Beeton. Beeton needed a new water system. The springs just above the hills to the south of the village would be a good source. The village needed money to develop the system. Robert was invited to Ottawa to speak with Prime Minister Sir Charles Tupper. He chose to take young Kate with him. Ann prepared more than sufficient food for the train ride to Ottawa and back as there was not food available on the train. This would be Kate's first trip to the nation's capital, a trip that she would recall time and time again on her many future visits to the Canadian Capital.

Much of the Scott's business was based on credit or bartered farm products for merchandise. Many of the farmers would have some cash in the late summer and early fall. This was the time of year that the wholesalers from Toronto were pushing for the money the Scott's owed them.

Robert took a number of days to go by horse and buggy to visit his many customers. His companion on the farm visits was often, young Kate. She loved it because it meant days off of school. It was a time where she got to know her Father better. On these days he talked of his love for her Mother. Kate came to realize that her Father, although he loved his children, had a passionate love for her mother that far surpassed his love for his children. He would tell Kate story after story about his amazing wife. On more than one occasion he concluded his story by telling Kate that she was a great girl but she would never be the woman that her Mother was.

Chapter 4

Ann Kennedy Scott

Mrs. A described her mother as the solid, steadying influence in the Scott home. She was firm and consistent in her discipline. Her firmness and discipline was always full of obvious love. She had been responsible for much of the upbringing of her younger brothers. Her mother was frail as her nerves gave her continuous problems. Ann had to grow up quickly. She loved excitement. She loved a party. She loved people. She would bubble over with excitement when she was organizing a time of hospitality in their home or in the community. Ann enjoyed each moment of life and passed this love on to her children.

The Beeton Fall Fair was the biggest event of the year. The store would have one of its busiest days of the year. The family table was crowded with friends and customers for the supper meal. Everyone wore their Sunday best to the fair. The kids could feel the excitement building each day as the fair approached. When they received their free admission passes the day before the fair from their school teacher, they were ready to go. All that was needed was the money that they hoped Father would give them for spending.

The fact that their mother was always a keen competitor in the baking competition only added to the excitement. They watched as their mother prepared her entries. They wanted to be among the first people to see the judge's decision when the agriculture hall opened around eleven. Ann won many red ribbons for her baking. There was seldom a year that she didn't earn at least a couple. These prize winners would become part of the feast that Ann served the very night of the fair.

When Ann discovered that the CNE had a women's section she became anxious to enter the five crafts that she could enter for less than a dollar. She spent a year working on her needle work and knitting. The finished products were taken from Beeton to Toronto by a trusted sales person who dealt with the Scott store.

On the first day of the exhibition Ann headed to Toronto on the Grand Trunk train with young Kate as her companion. Father had to look after the store. The train left Beeton early in the morning and would leave the Exhibition after the fireworks ended. It was a long and exciting day for young Kate. Little did she know that the exhibition would become an important part of her future life. The great thrill of that day was that her Mother won two red ribbons and a third prize as three of the five entries won prizes. Kate had heard of the exhibition even earlier in her life as D.A. Jones was a participant who won many ribbons for his honey.

Robert only kept the store books up to date when he had to. The receipts and bills would pile up on his desk until Ann would sternly tell her husband that he must get at the books.

Ann's great desire as a young girl was to become a teacher. Family circumstances had not allowed this to happen. Through the years many of the village's single teachers were boarded at the Scott house. Both Robert and Ann were always supportive of their children's teachers. Ann was always willing to help her children with homework when help was required.

Like her husband ,faith was very important to her. She was always a "Martha" when help was required. Her love of church music that was full of joy was shown by her regular Sunday night visits to the Methodist Church just a couple blocks down the street.

When Kate's Father, with love, had told her she would never reach the level on the pedestal that her Mother had attained, it made the future Mrs. A determined to reach that level- and even possibly a level above.

Chapter 5

Mrs. A's Younger Years

It was always an exciting time in the Scott household. The children's Mother, Ann, could make a time of cleaning up after a party or a large dinner gathering a fun adventure. The children enjoyed each other as well as their parents. The strict discipline was so tempered with love that the children appreciated being kept in line. It was not that Kate and her brothers and little sister were always obedient. They were a fun-loving group of youngsters.

The Riddells owned a farm behind the Scott store. The young children loved to play on the farm land. The big bush at the far end of the farm was great for wild berry picking, wild flower picking, and beechnut gathering. The hills provided a great avenue for sleigh riding.

Mr. Riddell was not always happy with the Scott children's activity on his farm, especially if he had a crop of corn planted in the field right behind the Scott store. One of the games that the kids loved to play was hide and seek amongst the corn stalks. This is a lot of fun for the participants but is not good for the farmer's corn crop.

Mr. Riddell had spoken to Robert about his children playing amongst the corn stalks. Robert promised Mr. Riddell that this would not happen again- but it did. One evening Mr. Riddell was at the Scott's door complaining that Robert's children had been out in the corn field. This was disobedience to their Father. Mr. Scott said that he would strap each child. Mr. Riddell felt that a strapping would soon be forgotten.

The two men discussed the punishment. As this was a Sunday evening, the store was closed and the children's Mother was at the Methodist Church. The punishment was that the children would have to stand straight up on the tall stools in the store until their Father allowed them to get off. Mr. Scott got a book to read as he sat in the store to make sure the children stayed on the stools. When his wife came home he went out to the house for a minute to explain to her what was happening. One of Kate's brothers suggested to her that she fall off her stool. Another brother said to this bother that he should fall off his stool. Jack, the first brother, said that it would be much more effective if Kate fell off her stool because Father would not want her to be hurt. She fell off her stool and was hurt when she hit her head causing blood to gush out from the cut. Father and Mother came rushing into the store. The gushing blood was much worse than the cut. Jack's plan did not include the cut but the plan worked. The punishment was over. Kate wrote in her book about Beeton of several other interesting happenings amongst the Scott children who loved to play and were not above getting into trouble as a result of this play.

Kate was found guilty of smuggling a book to school for the purpose of reading it when the teacher was involved with another class in the same room. The book was hid in her clothes. The book was discovered. Kate was chastised and immediately quit smuggling books to school for secret reading.

Kate loved to help her mother when she was baking. She was amazed that Mother could check the temperature of the oven by sticking her bare elbow into it. When the temperature was right the baking was placed in the oven to be perfectly cooked.

On Sunday afternoons after the noon meal dishes were washed and put away, Mr. Scott taught the children scripture and the catechism of the Presbyterian Church which included one hundred and seven questions. He would begin with, "What is the chief end of man?" The children would reply, "Man's chief end is to glorify God and to enjoy Him forever." At the evening anniversary church service, the choir usually began the service by leading the congregation in singing "All people that on earth do dwell sing to the Lord with cheerful voice."

Kate recounts that she always thought of St. Andrews when she heard this same Psalm being sung as she attended services in St. Giles, Edinborough, in Brussels, in South Africa, in Sydney Australia, and at St. Paul's Cathedral in London.

Chapter 6
Millinery Opening

This chapter is made up of excerpts directly from Mrs. A's book "Never a Day So Bright." The words speak for themselves.

One winter in New York not long ago, at the advance fashion showings, I saw the most amazing array of hats these eyes have ever viewed. The creations were by Sally Victor, and one of them caught the imagination of everyone present. Perched on the blonde head of the model was a bewildering confection of chiffon, plumes, rhinestones and veiling.

"Ah-h" sighed every one of the two hundred and fifty fashion writers assembled there, "Isn't it marvelous? Isn't it dashing? And so new!"

New? I had seen it, or its twin, fifty years before, sitting on the carefully waved hair of Mrs. D.A. Jones at the big spring Millinery Opening in my father's general store in Beeton, Ontario. Looking at that hat and the ostrich plumes, I felt as if I had been transported back to our country store with its great miscellany of shoes and dresses, ribbons and hardware, tea and cheese, that never failed to delight all seven of us children. But it was the millinery department that really entranced us, because there lay the romance of our small village, with its Millinery Openings spring and fall.

The dates of the Milliner Openings were as immutable as the seasons themselves. Spring hats were worn on Easter Sunday and not one day before. Fall hats got their first showing on the day the Beeton

Fall Fair opened during the first week of October. But before both those dates came weeks of frenzied preparation, since hats in those days were not casual, nor were they to be taken lightly. Each hat was a major production.

The Millinery was the key to success. When the Robert Scott store first opened its millinery department my father used to go to Toronto to select the milliner himself. Just as models are auditioned now, so the old-time milliner was auditioned in the Toronto wholesale millinery houses. But it wasn't long before Mother realized that our dad, devoted as he was to my mother, still was bowled over by a young, good-looking milliner. In most cases the milliner my father chose was more personable than sales- minded. And she loaded him up with more wire, buckram, velvet, feathers, flowers, and veiling than any small village could handle. So eventually it was our shrewd, smart and kindly mother who journeyed down to Toronto, forty-eight miles away, and selected the milliner, the merchandise and all the paraphernalia that went with the making of hats.

And what a journey it was! Mother stocked the house before she went as if we were being left shipwrecked on an island. Pies, layer cake, cold meat, homemade bread, everything was laid down ahead in the pantry.

At that time our nearest railway station was Bradford, twelve miles away. Mother packed her bag carefully; Father drove her to Bradford, and from there she took the train to Toronto. She was away three long days, and to us children the time seemed endless. But finally she arrived home again with an armful of parcels, a thousand tales about the magic city, and a gleam in her eye that meant she had snared a really good milliner.

For weeks on end parcels came into the store, since hats in those days were built from foundation up. If we were very good we were permitted just one look into the boxes. Chiffon, flowers, straws, velvet and plumes of every color! They fascinated us. The rolls of wire, wire snippers and buckram weren't too exciting, but they were part of the whole picture.

Around the first of March the milliner arrived, and now the whole tempo began to step up, for that was a social occasion in our village.

With her she brought what a Hollywood star brings today- glamor. She had smartly dressed hair, a voluptuous figure, and strange exotic perfumes.

The pressure was on. It needed, as well as the milliner, two or three apprentices to turn out the two or three hundred hats required for the Millinery Opening. They were local girls who lived at home, came in at eight o'clock in the morning, and worked all day making wire frames, cutting buckram, and sewing in pleated chiffon facings to match the straw. And then there was the binding on the velvet. That was where the first trouble arose. Velvet in those days was definitely crushable. All day the kitchen stove had to be almost red hot. When the velvet was crushed, down would come an apprentice, lift off the stove lid and lay over it a dripping wet flannel cloth. Then when the steam was rising, the velvet went on top of the steam, was whisked and brushed to all its original freshness.

The milliner had her own ideas of what was high style, but Mother, knowing every customer down to the last hair, knew far better what would sell and what price each customer would pay for a hat. Between them they effected a compromise- so many high-style bonnets, so many bread-and-butter models. The frenzied work of preparation went on, with hat after hat being made from its wire foundation right through to its last tiny curled plume. And in addition to all the work and preparation was all the worry about the Opposition (spelled with a capital because my Father was politically minded) across the street. The Opposition too had a good milliner. He too was as shrewd as my mother. He too knew to the the last dozen eggs and the last firkin of butter what every farm woman would give in exchange for a hat.

There was also the question of timing. The Millinery Opening lasted two days. It must come before Easter. It couldn't interfere with Good Friday. So finally the two rival stores compromised on the Wednesday and Thursday before Good Friday. Saturday? That was laid aside for the returns, and for customers who wanted not a new hat, but an old hat made over.

Tuesday night was pretty much an all-night session. Indeed, years later we went through precisely the same thing before opening day at

15

the Canadian National Exhibition. With the eye of a general, Mother allocated each one of us our specific jobs. The whole store had to be swept and dusted. Then when everything was immaculate, the stands for the hats were set up, and the merchandise graded according to price.

To us it was shocking that we had to go to school on Millinery Opening days. We could hardly stand it and gave mighty little attention to our schoolwork. We rushed home at noon to see if there were any customers in the millinery department. There weren't because dinner time in our village and in the country round about was a sacred hour, not to be skipped over lightly. Instead of the usual hearty dinner, we dined on salmon sandwiches and quarts of milk. If we were lucky, Mother sent a note to the teacher asking if we might come home at three o'clock, explaining with capital letters, "THIS IS THE DAY OF THE MILLINERY OPENING."

By two o'clock in the afternoon the farmers and their wives began to arrive, women looking excited, the farmers looking as if this were all "a lot of women's nonsense that doesn't mean anything." Butter, eggs, and chickens were carried in, weighed or counted, and the tally added up. Every farmer insisted that the tea, sugar, and cheese be bought first, and debited from the account. The wife was then given two or three or, in extreme cases, four dollars for the new hat. But four dollars was really tops. Up streamed the customers, climbing the narrow stairs to the second floor, to be met by the impresario of the occasion, the milliner.

Of all the milliners we had in and out of the house and the store, one stands out in my memory like a beacon. Twenty years later, when I went to see one of the Theda Bara motion pictures, I looked at that glorious creature on the screen and thought, "Where have I see that woman before?" Then I remembered- "But it's our Mrs. Gillespie!" And sure enough it was Miss Gillespie, feature for feature. Sleek black hair (pulled carefully over a "rat") slumberous eyes, a bosom that *was* a bosom, a tiny corseted waist and a sweeping skirt. Black satin our Miss Gillespie wore which shimmered with every step she took and revealed every line of a sensuous figure.

Imagine a rather dowdy and plain figured woman stepping into the presence of such a charmer. What she had meant to buy was a plain straw hat that could stand up under five years of wearing. When she left, she carried in her hat bag a bright red sailor with a black plume tucked coyly under one ear. She never dared show it to her husband until she reached home, and what the husband said we never found out. But what my Father knew was this; For weeks an extra dozen eggs and three or four pounds of butter came in to help pay the overdraft on the hat. Occasionally it took a fresh ham to complete the payment. And those items were never entered in my Father's day-book.

By four o'clock the elite of our village began to arrive- the doctor's wife, the bank manager's wife, the school teachers' wives, and best of all- the lawyer's wife from Tottenham, five miles away. That was a real triumph. But there we ran into trouble, because almost every one of them brought with her in a small paper parcel a bit of ribbon or two or three old ostrich plumes- treasures stored from previous hats that might be grafted to a new model. But our Miss Gillespie was smart. "Yes," she would say, "Of course we can replace them. Just let me see the plumes."

Down would rush one of the apprentices with the old bedraggled plume. Mother would be standing by with another hot stove- lid. Again the hot wet cloth, the steam rising in the kitchen- but this time, instead of a whisk, a silver knife was brought out. Shaking the plume over the steam, Mother would take each strand of the feather, pull it out gently, and curl it back over the dull side of the knife until it looked like new. My Father always thought this was really bad business, but my mother said, "Better that we should humor them than let them go to the Opposition."

Finally the first day was over. Miss Gillespie, the apprentices, my father, and all the clerks from the store would sink into their places around the huge dining-room table. And here was where my mother really did her stuff- hot scalloped potatoes, roast ham, lemon pie, layer cake, pots of strong green tea, homemade bread. We sat there and stuffed ourselves, not worrying a particle about the fact that we had dishes to wash up. For directly the meal was over our parents and Miss Gillespie would retire upstairs to the millinery showroom and add up the take. More than that, every sale was carefully calculated against the people who should have come in and didn't, and against the new customers we had taken away from the Opposition.

Thursday found us all pretty groggy, but game to go on to the end, because then, as now, there were always the late-comers who thought: "Today I must buy me a hat; else I can't go to church on Easter Sunday." And here our Miss Gillespie really showed her finesse. Carefully laid aside and not exhibited on the opening day were another fifty fresh hats, fresh, individual and new. And so the battle continues all day Thursday. It was a little complicated by the fact that some of the Wednesday customers came back, and wanted to start all over again.

Friday we rested briefly, getting ready for the makeovers that flooded into the millinery department on Saturday. The window shoppers who had been with us both Wednesday and Thursday, who had tried on every hat, some of them twice over, came in with relics of elegant contraptions they had bought in previous years. They knew my father was a soft-hearted Irishman. They knew all they needed to say was: "You know, Robert, this has been a pretty tough winter. And you know I paid three dollars for this hat three years ago. Surely you can do something about it." And Father, looking rather sheepish, would lead them up the stairway and there fling them on the hands of Miss Gillespie.

Finally, at midnight Saturday, the last customer walked out of the store. And then, while we children dragged off to bed, more dead than alive, our parents and Miss Gillespie sat down again and totaled up figures. We went to sleep with the murmur of: "Mrs. Smith wasn't in this year" or "I wonder what happened to Mrs. McDonald?"

But Sunday it was all fresh and new again. Scrubbed, slicked up, dressed in our Sunday clothes, we filed into our pew at the Presbyterian Church, The seven of us, in order of our ages, with my eldest brother at the head of the line. Mother and Father both sang in the choir. Then when church was over and dinner was finished we settled down for a real old-fashioned gossip. For on Easter Sunday Mother and Father were not so entranced with the sermon or the Easter hymns that they couldn't tell us to the last ribbon how many Scott hats were there, or how many hats of our Opposition flaunted their plumes in *our* church on Easter Sunday.

Sally Victor? Fifth Avenue? Shucks, Sally Victor will never have the same thrill out of a hat creation as did Miss Gillespie or my mother and dad, because every hat had a personal history. It represented so many dozen eggs, so many pounds of butter, so many chickens, and it would be a fresh ham or five pounds of spareribs thrown into pay for that extra ribbon.

Chapter 7
The Role of the Women

When one looks at the women of the Beeton community, there was family after family where the husband and wife worked side by side. This was always true on the farm. The couple supported one another. There really was not any money. There was very little travel. There was a multitude of joy and happiness in the family, in the community, and the community events.

There is an old saying which goes, "The hand that rocks the cradle rules the world." The mothers in the Beeton community that Kate grew up in were mostly of this sort. Outward appearances can be deceiving. It seemed that the men were completely in control. It seemed that the men had the freedom but in Kate's own words her Mother was the solid, steadying rock in the Scott family.

This was very true of the Scott household as one can easily see in the chapter on the milliner. The deep love of a man for a woman and the deep love of a woman for a man is something that mankind in the Christian world has been trying to understand for hundreds of years. It is difficult to understand why a widow will often live much longer than a widower. Robert may have come close to the actual source when he said to his daughter that she could never be the woman that her mother is.

Kate grew up in a home where a woman was highly respected in her own right. This was very important in the development of Mrs. A.

Chapter 8
Young Kate in a Changing World

The early 1900's was a time when Canadian society was beginning to go through some major transitions. The automobile, the radio and electricity would change life forever. World War I was a major factor in women receiving the right to vote. Women were becoming more involved in jobs and life outside of the home.

Mrs. A was always at the forefront in the changes that women were experiencing. This was not because she was involved in any political movement. She was not. It was not that she had any ax to grind. She did not. She was a strong human being who enjoyed life and who was her own self. When there was a problem, she was interested in solving it. When there was a challenge she was interested in taking up the reigns of that challenge and moving ahead. She was a born leader. She didn't force herself into leadership. She didn't have to. Her leadership was just part of the life that Mrs. A relished.

At sixteen years of age she went the twelve miles to Bradford for a three month course to become a qualified teacher. She had already supplied for a few days in the Beeton public school when one of the teachers was sick. Kate had a natural talent for teaching. Although she did not remain in the classroom for very long, she taught all of her life.

Coming from the Scott household she had a natural love of books as did her parents, her brothers, and sister. Her Grandmother Kennedy had come from Scotland where her grandparents helped run a bookstore. A book store was opened up in Guelph by these same grandparents, who were the great grand parents of young Kate. Kate was a good student, whose parents made sure that she kept to the task at hand.

Mrs. A's first teaching job was in Adjala Township just west of Beeton. The school had thirty eight pupils in the one room school. The eight grades of public school spanned the whole range of children from small grade one students to big boys in grade eight who failed two or three times and were even bigger than the teacher and not much younger. These boys were required to help on the farm. Farm work came before school attendance. As a result, many of them had the attitude that school was something you did when there wasn't anything else to do. Their attitude was that they were going to be farmers and book knowledge was not important.

Some of the bigger boys in the Adjala School had a reputation for harassing their teachers, resulting in the teacher soon leaving. Young Kate was aware of this situation. Before the school year began she purchased a strap. When the first of these boys lipped her, Kate took her strap, walked straight to the boy, and hit him as hard as she could. She never had to use the strap again.

After a very successful year, Kate had an opportunity to get a job in the Beeton School teaching just three grades. Her salary would rise from $325 a year to $375 a year and she would be at home. She taught in Beeton for two years, during which time she took another teachers course to upgrade her qualifications.

This was a time in Canada when the slogan "Go west young man, Go west" was very important. Realizing that "man" really meant all people Kate decided to head west. With her heritage from the Scott and Kennedy families this seemed like a very reasonable journey.

She got a job in Cypress Hills which is situated in south west Saskatchewan. It was a small school with thirteen students. School ran from April until early fall as the bitter cold of the Saskatchewan winter made travel to and from school on horseback next to impossible.

Her train trip out west was a four day journey on a colonist train. The train had wooden bunks and a stove in each car where a passenger could cook a meal. Kate would only be in Cypress Hill for six months before the news of her Father's impending death brought her back to Beeton.

Kate enjoyed her stay in the west. It was like a holiday. Book studying was not of great importance in this community where ranching was what life was all about. Although winter in Southern Saskatchewan can be quite harsh, the summer can be very pleasant especially in an area like Cypress Hills. Out of necessity, Kate became a horseback rider.

No one had told Kate that the school was three miles from the ranch where she would be living. She was certainly not aware that the only method of travelling to the school was on horseback. She came to realize this when three horses were led up to the kitchen door on the first day of school. She knew that two of the pupils she was to teach called the ranch where she was living home. The third horse was for her. She had no idea of how to mount the horse. She had no idea how she made it to school over the three miles, but she did. She met the other eleven students of the school who also arrived by horseback. Each and every one of these students had learnt to ride almost as soon as they could walk.

It only took to recess time for Kate to learn that she needed a saddle of her own. There were plenty of extra horses for her to choose one to ride, but each person had their own saddle. One of the trustees arranged for her to buy a saddle for $60. Kate could pay for the saddle by the trustees withdrawing ten dollars a month from her pay. Another's rancher's wife made her a divided riding skirt. She discovered on her first adventure to the school that a tight suit skirt would not work.

It was not long before Kate could ride with her students and the adult people at the ranch. She rode the range and she shot coyotes. Neighboring dances were great events. The semiannual shopping spree of her host family to Maple Creek took a day's travel with the mother and smaller children travelling in the wagons while Kate and the older children rode on horseback. The shopping expedition to the one general store brought many happy memories of Beeton and her father's store.

Chapter 9
Home Life Changes

The death of Robert Scott meant that Ann and her daughter Kate would take over the running of the store. The older brothers were already in the work world or at university. Her young sister was still in school and her youngest brother had just begun working at the bank.

The store that the two women began running at the end of the first decade of the 20th century was not the same Scott's Store of Kate's early childhood. With the changing times, the people of the area were becoming more mobile. Train travel was increasing. Some automobiles were coming to the village and Simpsons and Eatons Catalogues were becoming competition for the neighborhood stores. Bartering was still significant but was declining as more people were beginning to work for wages.

Another major factor was that Mr. Scott's health had been declining. This meant that the vigor with which he brought in new and different merchandise had declined. Much of the store's inventory was old. There were debts that needed to be paid. There was money that needed to be collected. The ladies had major sales to clean out the old stuff. Enough money was raised to clean off the debts but their buggy runs to the farmers in the area were not as successful as the runs that Kate and her father had made. Kate also had a job as supply teacher in her former public school.

Kate's brother Bruce had become quite successful in the insurance and real estate business in Alberta. He came home and suggested that the store should be sold. He offered his mother and sister an expense paid trip to the west coast of Canada and the United States. Mother Ann was not sure, but became convinced especially when it was suggested that the family home should be moved to Toronto where most of the children were in school or working.

Ann was able to become the housekeeper for her grown children in their new residence. Kate got a job teaching at a school with over twenty other teachers. In their spare time the grown Scott children enjoyed skating, tennis, and the brand new silent movie theatre.

At the very traditional Presbyterian Church the family attended, a problem arose when a number of the younger women wanted to use part of the church hall as a gymnasium to participate in some fitness exercises. The minister was in agreement but a number of the older members did not like the idea at all. Eventually the minister prevailed. An instructor was hired and the work-outs took place.

When Kate had returned to Beeton from Cypress Hill, Henry Aitken and she began to see more of each other. During the winter that she was in Toronto the two became engaged. While Kate was in Toronto, Henry had gone west to a mining town in Minnesota in search of new adventure.

Their wedding took place the next fall. The young couple left immediately for Virginia, Minnesota which was a small mining town in an area where there were many similar little towns.

Chapter 10
The Return to Beeton

The stay in Minnesota lasted almost two years. During that time Kate lost a baby as a result of small pox. The majority of the population in the small mining towns were immigrants from lands where English was not spoken. Kate helped out in the local library, supply taught, and helped arrange Sunday afternoon record concerts.

When Henry returned to Beeton for a month because of his brother's illness, Kate made Christmas cakes that she sold in the neighborhood. Henry's brother had been running the family flour mill in Beeton. When he passed away, Henry and Kate returned to the village so that Henry could run the mill.

Across the street from the mill was twenty-six acres of land. The Aitkens decided to buy this land and make it the family homestead. Henry ran the mill. Kate began developing the twenty-six acres into Sunny Bank.

The location was ideal. It was across the street from the mill. It was situated on the west edge of the village. The fairgrounds where the Beeton Fall Fair was held was the property directly to the east of Sunny Bank. Going out the front lane from the property, the two young daughters who were born to Kate and Henry, Mary and Anne, just had to walk across the street to the Beeton Public and Continuation School. Going out the same lane the family could walk or drive less than a block and a half away to Saint Andrews Presbyterian.

The property was great for Kate to develop the prize chickens that she wished to have. It was ideal to develop some apple orchards, so much so that a later owner would name the property Appledel. There was room for the planting of berry bushes and to develop a large potato field. Kate did not know it at the time but the potato field would become one if the village's most significant areas in providing work for a number of the village's adults and children for many decades.

Kate was very busy in the life of the community. With her sister-in-law, she began a youth choir at St. Andrews. There were forty two members in this choir ranging in age from eight to sixteen. In its beginning the choir members wore their own Sunday clothes but as the choir began to sing at special church services and began taking engagements outside the church, there was a growing need for a choir uniform. This resulted in a uniform of black dickies, white surplices and black tams.

To raise money for the uniforms the choir produced the cantata "The Fairy Shoemaker". Fathers made the props for the show and mothers made the costumes. With each choir member having at least ten relatives, the show was a great success. There was enough money to buy the material for the dickies and the surplices. Members of the Ladies Aid came to the Aitken home to make the clothing. The velvet caps were purchased in their finished form.

The choir practiced on Friday evenings. There was usually a birthday or two to celebrate. This meant that there was a chocolate cake and birthday candles as well as hot cocoa to drink. The young choir members were in the mood to sing when they finished this treat.

Her desire to help woman reach their full potential took a big step forward when she became a leader in forming the local Women's Institute. She became its first president. Kate would go on to be an important part of the provincial organization. In the early 1920's she served as the provincial agricultural convener. The Women's Institute had begun in the last decade of the 1800's. Its first purpose was to educate farm women on health and hygiene to help them raise a healthy family. The Institute also encouraged women to get together to share their lives and develop their household skills into crafts that were helpful in fundraising for the community, the province, the country, and even the world.

Women had just received the right to vote. World War I was over. The war had made it necessary for many women to take up jobs that had been left with no workers when the men went off to war. When the men returned, a number of the women continued to work at the jobs where they were employed during the war.

The roaring twenties were coming. The economy was booming. The 1920's saw the formation of the United Church of Canada. The United Church was formed from a union of the Methodist, Congregational, and Presbyterian Churches. Although the leaders of the churches were in an agreement, there was not unity amongst the members. This was especially true of the Presbyterian membership. Many villages and towns across Canada found themselves at the centre of the dispute. Sometimes it even became a family split.

The village of Beeton found itself in the middle of one of these disputes. Although there were members of St. Andrews who went to the former Methodist church on Centre Street, there were many who would not go. They were Presbyterians and were going to remain Presbyterians.

Kate was always interested in a cooperative community. This was not possible during this dispute. The Scott and Aitken traditions were deeply bound in the Presbyterian tradition. The Aitkens were not prepared to leave St. Andrews. Like, Dr.S.R. McKelvey, who became a dear friend of Kate's, Kate would spend her life as a member of the Presbyterian Church. Dr.McKelvey would be one of those who spent his life at St. Andrews but saw members of his own family attend the United Church.

Chapter 11

Kate - The Perfectionist

As a member of a family whose mother and father both believed that any job worth doing was worth doing well, Kate was taught throughout her growing years to be excellent in all that she did. Kate believed that what her parents were teaching was correct.

She saw her father make a special blend of tea to sell in the store. She saw how every ingredient of the tea was measured so that the correct amount was in the tea. She saw the people who were invited to taste test the tea. If the taste was not correct, there were changes made in the ingredients. When the tea passed all tests it could be sold.

Kate and her brothers were part of the team who prepared the excess of the store's butter for shipment to Toronto. The Scott's received many, many pounds of butter from their customers in exchange for products that the customer needed from the store. There was much more butter bartered for grocery and hardware products than the store could ever sell. The butter was of many different qualities. Some of the farmers made good butter. Others made butter that was of lesser quality. The job of the Scott family was to take all of the excess butter and work it over so that the quality was a standard quality that the market in Toronto would buy. When the butter reached the stage of being ready to send to Toronto, the Scott children assisted in packaging it.

Spring cleaning of the store and the house was a well-organized family venture. Ann Scott was the person in charge. Everyone helped.

When the cleaning was completed to Ann's satisfaction, not only the table in the kitchen was clean to eat off of, but the floors too could have been a dinner plate. Every toilet basin, every cupboard and every crack in the floor shone brightly. The cleaning was perfection. As Kate has stated, her mother was capable of making something like the cleaning of the house, into a festive occasion so that the children did not think of it as a task but as an event to be enjoyed.

When Ann Scott decided to enter five of her hand crafted pieces into the CNE competition, she spent hours and days during the winter, spring, and summer to make, remake, and remake again the crafts. That is why she won the two red ribbons. Kate observed her mother's work. When the young girl went with her mother to see the results at the fair, she was impressed not only with the results; she was impressed by the process.

It was observing her parents and the favorable results that they both experienced from their diligence to achieve excellence that was a major factor in Kate's approach to her own life.

Chapter 12
The Hens and Potatoes

The main reason that Henry and Kate bought the twenty-six acres was the vision that Kate had to develop a top quality chicken flock that would lay some of the best eggs ever produced. As a young girl she had observed and heard stories of D.A. Jones and what he had done to produce some of the best honey in the world.

She received advice from government and agricultural college experts. Kate used the most up to date methods that she could find. It was necessary to systematically cull chickens from the flock. This was necessary in spite of the fact that the chickens she bought were from registered breeding stock. The egg that each hen laid was recorded. Kate was glad to have the government inspectors come to see what she was doing.

The chickens were fed only the very best. Kate grew green oats. These green oats provided her chickens with necessary minerals. This lady knew her hens. It was not every hen that received these green oats. It was only the very best of the hens, the ones whose records were at the highest level. In cold weather, Kate was known to have fed cod liver oil and vitamins by hand to the very best of the hens.

After a decade, two of her hens set world egg- laying records for their breed. It was the same year, 1927 that Kate went to Ottawa for an International Poultry Congress. She took a dozen of her Wyandotte hens. Her chicken stock was becoming well known not only in North America but also in Britain.

In her book "Making your Living is Fun", Kate wrote the following.

When our largest order —for 1000 pullets —came in from the British Department of Agriculture we walked on air. Condition of the sale was that the pullets be passed and graded by both Canadian and British government inspectors.

One day late in August that inspection was completed. Every bird was perfect, every bird banded. There remained only the shipment of the pullets, after which the government cheque would be forwarded. That night I was completely happy, but had no one with whom to share my delight. My husband was off on a business trip, my two small daughters were away on holiday, and none of our help slept in. But my happiness was only a matter of hours.

Just before dawn the little beagle hound sleeping on the porch whined in such a distressed way that he wakened me. As I opened the door to let him in I saw a man running down the lane towards the gate. With a premonition of disaster I ran to the pullet pen. The empty roosts, the sweetish, heavy odor of chloroform still hanging in the air, meant only one thing-the theft of our pullets ready for shipment.

While I pulled on a few clothes, the idling of the truck at the gate quickened to a roar and it pulled away. Our little farm truck was standing in the driveway; I jumped in and gave chase for four miles, but in my heart I knew there wasn't a hope of catching them, so I turned back. The sun was rising, but far more vivid was the blaze in the sky over what I knew was our home. My heart stopped beating; not only had the pullets been stolen but the pen fired. Freshly strawed for the inspection, it burned like tinder; nothing could have stopped the blaze.

Our village constable alerted the city police forty-eight miles away, but it was too late. In the opinion of the police the truck and the registered poultry were over the border before anyone could trace them. Stunned by the blackened ruins and my withered hopes, I walked round in a daze for a week.

When we first bought our land, the agricultural experts said, "You know Kate, that south slope, with a little feeding, will be ideal land for an apple orchard-and stick to Northern Spies and MacIntoshes."

We had planted eight acres in young apple trees; and since I was young, waiting eight years for a Mac crop and 15 years for a Spy harvest didn't worry me one particle; but in the meantime the land had to pay for itself. In between the young trees we planted buckwheat, and to enrich the soil plowed it under when it grew. After two years the land was good enough to grow early potatoes. How to get those potatoes on the market when they would bring $5.00 a bag was the problem. Again I went to the Agricultural College for advice. Early potatoes need heat for early sprouting, and by this time we had four Jersey cows in the stable, all giving off body heat. "Why not utilize that warmth?" said my advisors.

During the winter we made long wire racks and hung them from the beams over the heads of the cows. Seed potatoes were bought, cut for planting and the raw edges dusted with lamp-black to seal in the moisture. Up they went, single layers on every rack, and were left there to sprout. At first our temperamental Jerseys distrusted this overhead; but every time any of the cows tossed her head and breathed heavily upward, more potatoes sprouted. Before planting time arrived everyone in the neighborhood had heard of this madcap adventure. "Just another example, "said the experienced farmer, "of fools rushing in where angels fear to tread. Those potatoes will rot before she ever gets them planted.

They didn't rot, but sprouted beautifully. Since our soil was light and the spring unusually early, we were able to plant April 14th. It was a slow job since the potatoes couldn't be tossed in casually but had to be placed sprouts up. So, as well as the family, we had to employ six men. Need I say the planting proceeded with plenty of spectators on the sidelines giving all kinds of free advice?

It was a dull day, with heavy clouds overhead threatening rain. There was even the occasional light shower. But we finished at five o'clock in the afternoon. Then occurred one of the human incidents always remembered. Said one of our small daughters, gazing skywards as the last row was covered: "Now, God let her rain!"

The spring weather was ideal. The potatoes grew fast and so did the potato bugs; it was spray, spray all the time. But as the tops began to wither again I indulged in my "sup positioning", book keeping. Even at $4.00 a bag the bank overdraft would be slimmed down.

We ordered in the potato digger, got bags and weigh scales, and started to harvest the crop. That was a big day for the village. On the hill across the road from us sat the local wiseacre with a pair of binoculars, counting the bags. We trucked the crop to market forty-eight miles away, only to find that every vegetable gardener in the more southerly part of the province was also trucking in early potatoes. Almost overnight the bottom dropped out of the market. Instead of $4.00 a bag we got 75cents, less 12 per cent selling commission. Had it not been for the unpaid labor of the family we would have been in the red. The only black in evidence was the lamp-black, which had settled on both ceiling and walls of the stable. We had to whitewash it.

Chapter 13
A Business Woman and a Spokeswoman

Although the hens were the dominant part of the farm at Sunny Bank, they were far from being the only product of the farm. Henry raised dogs. There were cows to be milked. Although the apple trees were not big enough to produce a harvest the potato fields, the vegetable garden, and the berry bushes did provide a yearly harvest.

The potatoes, the beans, the milk from the cows, and the abundance of berries were much more than the little family could consume. And of course, there were the eggs. Kate had begun a weekend delivery of eggs and roasting chickens to Toronto city customers. When she began taking some loaves of homemade bread and some butter churned from the milk of the family cows, Kate found that she had customers asking about the possibility of other products such as cookies, pies, and cakes.

Farm vegetables in the 1920's did not have a very long time life of freshness. The season was short. Kate decided that the best way to make money out of the vegetables was to can them. She set up a home canning factory in her basement. During the harvest time, local women were hired to pick and preserve the vegetables. Kate's weekend hampers continued to increase in size. It was not long until Kate expanded her business to include restaurant and specialty stores in her Toronto market: in one year she sold 120,000 jars of produce.

Because Kate always insisted in working closely with the government officials on the development of her chickens, the officials became very aware of the type of work that Kate was doing in the agricultural world. These officials were not aware of many other women who were involved in agricultural experiments like Kate. As a result, when the government decided that in the developing world of womanhood that it wanted to have a government spokeswoman talking to women across the province and in Canada, the name of Kate Aitken was at the top of the list.

In 1921 Kate was asked to go about the province to talk to groups and give seminars in the area of agriculture that she was familiar with. She spent six weeks in the summer and six weeks in the winter on these tours. She traveled by train, by developing automobiles, by mail wagon, by carriage, and by sleigh.

Her audience was primarily the women who were already getting involved in the Women's Institute. Kate continued with this work for six years hiring help in Beeton to do her work and look after the children when Henry was busy at the mill. In Kate's report to the government in 1924, she wrote of how women were working with the agricultural reps to cull hens that were not producing. She cited the example of a group on Manitoulin Island who the previous summer had culled 3,000. These were shipped to market giving the owners cash for the birds that were little value to the farmer. It was also saving on feed.

The English delegation that Kate had met at the International Poultry Congress in 1927 in Ottawa thought that it would be good to have Kate to head up a Canadian exhibit to the London craft event that they were organizing for the countries of the British Empire the following year.

She went. Her continuing relationship with the Women's institute led her to be asked to take a bedspread which was in the Canadian exhibit to present it to the Duchess of York. It had been made by members of the Institute from the Province of Quebec. The bedspread was made from flax that had been spun by these ladies.

The Canadian exhibit was beside a booth that was run by cousins of the Duchess. The cousins arranged for the young Canadian girl to go to tea with the Duchess. Little did Kate know at the time, that the Duchess of York and her husband ,the Duke of York (who was at the tea) would become King George VI and Queen Elizabeth. This tea was also the first time that Kate would see in person the future Queen Elizabeth II, who was a toddler in the room.

Chapter 14

The Family is Always First

When Kate was growing up in the Scott household, father and mother shared the responsibility of the store, the home, and the upbringing of the children. Father Robert certainly was the central figure in the store but he could never have survived without Ann's contributions and advice. Ann was definitely the person in charge of the house. She received Robert's support. The children were raised by both Father and Mother. The family structure in the Scott household was very similar to that which existed for many farm families. Most of the entertainment for leisure time was found in the community and home. There was very little cash available in any household.

By the time Kate and Henry were raising their two daughters there were a number of changes taking place. Although there were still large families, most families were smaller in number than the families that their parents grew up in. This was true in the case of Kate and Henry. More young men and woman were involved in work outside of the home structure than in previous generations. The world of communication and travel was beginning to expand thanks to improvements in the phone, the radio, and the development of the automobile.

In the developing Canada more women were beginning to take an active part in community and Canadian affairs. There is no better example of this than the mother of the two young Aitken girls. Through her work in agriculture and the Women's Institute Kate was becoming a well-known figure.

This lady stated that the family needs must always be put first. She said that she was never an ambitious woman and had no desire to be a world beater. After six years of working for the Department of Agriculture spending six weeks in the summer and six weeks in the winter on the job, she quit the job to spend even more time than she had already been spending with her daughters, Mary and Anne, and her husband. The team of four worked together at Sunny Bank.

When she was on the job, she had worked Monday to Friday. She always brought presents home for the girls. The family spent time on the weekends sharing what had gone on in their lives that week. Kate always had time to read with the girls. On Sunday there was always church and Sunday school at St. Andrews. One of Kate's favorite stories about Sunday school was the day that the girls came home quite upset by the Sunday school lesson. The teacher had been describing the millennium. There was a great graphic description of the last trumpet, the opening of the graves, and the rising of the dead. They asked their mother if it was going to be like that. Kate assured the girls that would be more of an exciting, happy time like the fall fair with it bands playing joyful music. Anne then asked her mother whether she would be making the speech or would it be God?

Chapter 15
Here Comes the Ex

According to the CNE archives, it was 1923 that Kate became involved personally with that great fair. From her earlier trips to the fair she concluded that it needed above anything else an old fashioned country kitchen. She felt that there was much more at the fair for the rural men than there was for the women.

She rented a small booth space in the women's building. She had her bottled jams, jellies, and pickles for sale. There were freshly baked rolls, cakes, and pies. With their fresh aroma, the kitchen was an instant success. Kate's ability to communicate shone through as she shared the everyday tips on canning and preserving that she had discovered first at her mother's side in the family kitchen and those which she had then added through her home canning factory.

Kate's adventure of the Old Country Kitchen was so successful that the CNE directors asked her to conduct a cooking school during the Ex. An area on the Fashion Court of the old women's building was set aside for the school. However a fashion show preceeded the cooking school. While the props for the fashion show were wheeled off the stage, the pre-heated stoves, refrigerators, sinks, kitchen table, and kitchen cupboards were being carried on stage from the other side.

The building was old. It lacked proper wiring and plumbing. The cables for the electricity ran across the floor. A dry well was placed under the stage for drainage. Every time that the sink was brought on stage; it had to be properly connected to the dry well by a plumber.

Such conditions were normal in the public buildings in the late 1920's. It was necessary for Kate to concentrate on the show while at the same time keeping in mind the wires criss- crossing at her feet. On one occasion a plumber was still hooking up the drain under the stage when some water was poured into it. Kate ignored the language coming from below the stage. The show carried on.

By 1927, the audience for her show filled the entire building for every show. When the new electrical building was completed in the expanding horizons of the CNE Kate was asked to move her show to this building by the manufacturers of kitchen equipment. They felt the show would help sell their products.

The theatre seated twelve thousand people in a semi-circle. The theatre was surrounded by aisles of manufacturers, who were promoting their most recent kitchen appliances. Kate was assisted in her presentation by 12 helpers. The majority were university students. These twelve eager helpers swept out the theatres, peeled vegetables, and were known to love to lick the cake bowls clean.

The daily show was at 2 o clock. As the time of the show approached the helpers changed into white outfits. In these new clean clothes they handed out programs while helping the audience to their seats. Clothing was changed again before they assisted Mrs. A in presenting the program.

Kate showed her wise understanding of the human race as she featured many give- a ways and prizes. Freshly baked pastry was a great favorite, much like many large grocery stores give samples of products to their customers today. Audience members often had to wait in line for a few minutes for the next batch of the heated food.

The three main prizes at each show were a silver plate given to the newest bride present, a silver tray to the person who had come the furthest, and a mouthwatering three tiered birthday cake for the oldest person in the audience. More than one dispute had to be settled, as the participants at the show loved the silver tray and would argue that the mileage that had been traveled by her was greater than the mileage that someone else had travelled. It is said that some seventy year olds gained ten to fifteen years of age during the course of the show in order to win the cake.

There were few birth certificates carried in the 1920's. Driver's licenses were part of the world that was developing. And of course road maps were not important. There really was no practical way of showing the mileage travelled, nor the age; human nature is what it is.

The exhibition lasted a little over two weeks. During this time Kate's growing daughters were not far from their mother. They were able to enjoy the exhibition even more than Kate was able to on the first day when she had come to the fair with her mother.

Chapter 16

Changing Times

When Kate retired from her job of traveling twelve weeks of the year through the Canadian farm country, she was far from retired from public life. She was just getting her feet wet at the exhibition. She accepted the trip to the fair in England, and a couple years later to a World's Fair in Chicago. She had been contracted by an agricultural magazine which had already printed some of her reports of her travels.

This agricultural magazine provided further funds when she went to London. Kate was able to visit a number of European countries and write reports of various types of farming in Europe for her audience in Canada. The next year the federal agricultural department financed her trip as their representative to a wheat conference in London.

Through the Agricultural Minister from Italy, whom she became acquainted with, she was introduced to Benito Mussolini, the Italian dictator. The introduction made it possible for her to get an interview with him. It is quite possible that Mussolini was so impressed by the lady that he was willing to talk with her. It is possible that a male would not have gotten the interview and is even further possible that he did not even realize that he was being interviewed. Kate also returned from Italy with an order for Canadian wheat.

The year 1929 was on the horizon. The Great Depression was just around the corner. When it came, the Henry Aitken family was affected as were most Canadians. The flour mill was losing money. Western

Canada was entering a major drought that saw wheat crops dry up. Kate's luxury canning business began losing customers. The Aitkens had built up reserves of money but these reserves began to dwindle. When an advertising firm in Montreal asked her to do thirteen weeks of cooking school she quickly agreed. The family needed the money.

The year was 1932. The Aitkens were approaching twenty years of marriage. Kate was 41. The daughters were quickly becoming young ladies. The cooking classes took place each morning in movie theatres. The classes were demonstrations like the ones that are available to watch on TV in the twenty first century. The format was to demonstrate, instruct, and entertain. The sponsor was a branch of the Ogilvie Flour Company whose products were front and center at each presentation.

The success of the Montreal cooking school led to five years of these schools throughout Canada. The growing success of the weeks at the Ex each year was an added bonus for this development.

The year was 1934. Kate was putting on a school in Fredericton. The lead lady announcer on the radio broke her leg. The station manager needed an immediate replacement. He asked, and even begged a little to get the visiting celebrity cook to do her show live on the radio. Kate agreed. A few months later, Kate began her career at CFRB in Toronto. The position would last for the next 23 years.

Chapter 17

An Interlude

By 1938 most of Kate's time required her to be in the Toronto area. Henry had taken on a partner in the mill. In 1938, he sold his remaining shares in the mill to his partner. Kate and Henry moved to Long Branch on the western edge of the ever expanding Toronto.

Beeton was no longer her physical home, but her heart and her influence would always be there. The Canadian Exhibition has an interesting connection. D.A. Jones put his honey and Beeton on the map at the Exhibition. Kate was impressed by this. When her mother won her red ribbon in the early days of the women's program Kate was present.

It was Kate's idea to take an old country kitchen to the Ex for women to have more to do during their day at the Ex. In 1928 Beeton's band, - yes, Beeton's band, won the gold medal in their section of the Ex.

Kate would always have a pass to the Ex from 1923 until her passing. Her good friend, Dr. McKelvey, received a pass when he became a director at the Ex in his own right. As a young boy, your author was always impressed by the fact that Dr. McKelvey's car always had a pass on it at Ex Time.

Your author always had a love of the Ex, like Mrs. A. He has missed attending the Ex only one year since 1960. When he became the Provincial Secretary of Ontario Baseball, he was astounded to discover that one of his responsibilities was to be a member of the CNE pee wee baseball committee. His eyes were almost popping out of his head when he attended his first meeting in 1976. He was even more astounded to discover that he had a pass to the Ex. In 2013 he still is part of the committee. He still has a pass.

And so a person with Beeton roots has had a pass to the Ex. for over ninety years. Jimmy Rutherford's mother and Father attended, as guests, the CNE sports luncheon on the second Saturday of the Ex, for almost two decades. This is one of the events that Kate helped initiate and organize.

It was said in the 1950's, the 60's, and the 70's that the Beeton Fall Fair black and white show (Holstein) was certainly bigger than the show at the Ex., and probably surpassed that of the Royal Winter. It was because of the presence of the McCagues farm from Alliston, and the Cerswell Farm from Bond Head. The son of Charley Cerswell, the original owner of the farm, -Jimmy Cerswell is very active in the Beeton sports community as is the farm's herdsman's daughter, Phyllis Woodrow.

Kate loved the Beeton Fair and returned on a number of occasions to officially open it and would be impressed to find the next generation of farmers still very much involved with her community.

Kate's mother often referred to a very small scar on her daughter's face. She said the scar was from a cinder that landed on her face when she was a baby. She was being carried from the burning store where she had been born by one of the volunteer firemen. Much of Beeton's business section was destroyed by this fire including that store. It is interesting that John Wesley, the founder of the Methodist movement in the Christian Church, had a similar experience as a small boy in England when the manse that the family lived in was destroyed by fire.

Kate was born into a family that were strong believers in their Presbyterian church. She would be buried from a Presbyterian church eighty one years later. One of the important doctrines of the church is pre- destination. As the life of Kate is studied, a person cannot help wondering if she was born with a golden spoon in her mouth, or was she in fact, pre-destined to be the person that she became.

There is no question that she was always a hard worker, that she believed in sticking to the task at hand, and that she was always prepared to take advantage of an opportunity when it came her way. Her life shows these attributes time after time after time.

Chapter 18

A Real Blessing

The 1930's were not a pleasant time in rural Ontario. There were many women living in areas that had little communication with the outside world. The fact that Kate grew up in this rural Ontario gave her an understanding of the everyday problems that these women faced. Her travel for the Department of Agriculture in the 1920's added to this understanding. Her continuous work with the Women's Institute helped the women listening to Kate's broadcasts over CFRB to accept her for who she was. She was one of them. She was their voice.

Kate took her audience seriously. The program was a combination of household hints, gossip, and current events. Kate was a bright spot in the day. Radio was often the only entertainment in the home. Although there were a growing number of famous names on the radio, the average woman was often more impressed by the girl from next door. Kate was bringing the outside world into their home.

It was time to sit down with a cup of tea, a cookie or muffin and relax. It was time to hear what Kate had to say. It was a time to listen to a neighbor who was a good cook, and a neighbor who could share with you what was happening in the world out there. This was a neighbor who knew important people and was willing to share a wee bit of what those people were like.

Kate had an instinct for news. It often seemed that she was aware of the news before it happened. Her interest was not the story by itself.

She was interested in the human element of the story. Kate looked for a women's point of view, a human interest story, a fashion happening or the family behind the story.

When the Moose River Mine disaster happened in Nova Scotia in 1936, where the big story was the ongoing attempt to rescue three miners trapped by a landslide in a long shaft of an old mine, Kate's story began after two of the men were rescued. Kate's focus was on the people who were directly involved. She was able to bring to her listeners the stories of the people rescued and the stories of their family members. The imagination of the radio listeners would take them right to Nova Scotia and the Moose River area.

Kate prepared her own scripts. She had to get the material and the sources. By 1938, she had a staff that included nine secretaries. She had a contract with the Tamblyn drug stores. She worked out of their offices on Jarvis Street. However, when she accepted the appointment as Director of Women's Activity for the CNE it became necessary to move her office from the first of April until after Labor Day(the closing day of the Ex.), to the Women's Building at the Ex. Her staff was very busy. Under Kate's supervision, the two daily broadcasts, newspaper articles, and the organization of the women's activity for the coming fair all had to be coordinated each day.

During the Ex, Mrs. A's daily programs were one hour each. They originated in the Coliseum. One was in the afternoon and the other was in the evening. These broadcasts included news of the events at the Ex. that were happening or were going to happen the next day or the day after that. There were travel tips for those who would be coming to the Ex. There were daily interviews of the people who were involved with the Exhibition, again emphasizing the human element. There were interviews of famous people who were at the Exhibition on that day. The Duke of Kent, Duchess Juliana of the Netherlands, the wife of Count Mountbatten and the wife of the President of the United States, Eleanor Roosevelt, were but a few of these people.

Chapter 19

Loyalty

When the hour long radio shows were taking place Horace Lapp played the organ which connected one segment of the show to the next. Cy Strange was the announcer. Horace Lapp was the organist on Kate's first radio show. He was the organist on her last production twenty three years later. Cy Strange was one of only three announcers that the show had.

Kate was always a loyal person and she inspired this loyalty in others. Her brothers and sister were always very close in spite of the miles that often separated them. When Kate's father died, Kate came home to help her mother. When the store was sold Ann Scott was quite content to go to Toronto and be the main housekeeper for most of her children who were in Toronto. Henry and Kate came home from Minnesota to run the family mill when Henry's brother died. Kate worked her staff hard but treated each person fairly. She was like her mother- she could take a pile of work and make it into a fun time.

Whenever Kate was not home on a weekend when the two girls were growing up, their mother always communicated with them. As the years went by and the girls became women on their own, their very busy mother made sure that she talked every Sunday to each daughter regardless of where Mrs. A was on her world travels. When Kate had university students to help produce her early exhibition shows, some of them were friends of Mary and Anne who looked forward to assisting their mother.

There was no greater bond of loyalty developed than the one established in the early 1920's when Kate helped form Beeton Women's Institute. The mutual respect that Kate had for the members of the Institute, and that the members felt for her can be seen in event after event that took place in her life.

And then there is Beeton. There was scarcely a week went by on her radio program that the village did not receive a mention. Of course most of her audience loved it because most of their roots were found in a similar little town like Beeton. Kate continued to visit Beeton. She was there to open the fall fair. She was there for significant municipal events. She remembered her home church at St. Andrews. She visited her longtime friends when she came to town.

And then there was the love of her life, Henry. She left Ontario to go with Henry. She came back when his family loyalty brought him back to the village. The two worked side by side for over twenty years developing Sunny Bank and raising their two girls. Henry was usually there with the girls when Kate began travelling. Henry helped plant the apple trees and the berry bushes. It is interesting that when Kate's work took her to Toronto, Henry's work in Beeton was coming to a close. They moved to Long Branch. The two daughters were fully blossomed young women. Then home was just Kate and Henry.

Kate was seldom at home because of her schedule that just got busier and busier. Henry was not really a city person. His work as an accountant, took him to Kapuskasing. If he had been in Toronto, he would have spent most of his time by himself in a city environment that was foreign to him. The bond between Henry and Kate had grown through the years. They understood each other. Society often forgets that as each created individual is unique, each and every marriage is unique. What is one marriage's poison is another marriage's medicine.

When Henry retired, he retired to the new Sunny Bank that the family had bought at Streetsville, the name itself reflected the connection with the past. In later years, Kate was asked for advice for career women. Kate is quoted in the Toronto Star, *"regardless of why they have to work, or how long, they should always put the needs of their family at the top of the list. I think there's a great difference between a mother going to work to buy her baby new shoes and to buy a twenty one inch television set. It's difficult to say where necessity ends and luxury begins."* Mrs. A went on to say *"I can truthfully say that my career has never hurt my children, my husband, or myself. That is most important, believe me."*

Chapter 20

Her Father's Daughter

During World War I, Henry and Kate spent much of their time in Minnesota. As the U.S.A. did not join the war effort until 1917, the Aitkens were not in a war atmosphere. When they returned home, their concerns were on running the flour mill, developing their home, and beginning to raise a family.

World War II was entirely different. Kate had travelled much of the western world. She had met a number of world leaders. Above all else she had vivid memories of her Father and his lifelong obsession with the military. She recalled his work with the militia. His concern with the Boer War had etched a memory with Kate when she was just ten years old. The dashing figure of her father in military dress whenever there was an occasion for dressing up was a reminder to her of her handsome father.

During World War II, this father's daughter placed the war effort front and centre in all of her endeavors. When the Ex opened in 1941, Britain was staggering under continuous bombardment. Sections of major cities were destroyed. The people were homeless. Kate organized the setting up of a hundred old sewing machines in the Women's Division. The lady who had been one of the chief judges of the handicrafts for many years, Miss Helen Creighton, became the director of the women at these machines.

Through groups such as the Women's Institute, a hundred different volunteers came each day to sew. Each day the new volunteers had a different British city that they were trying to help with the items that were sewn that day. It is interesting that a project with different volunteers each day was not only good for Britain; it was also good for the Ex.

Many of the war service organizations and many of the volunteer organizations had leaders who visited the Ex for the major purpose of promoting the war effort which included relief effort. Mrs. A was usually the hostess to these people while they were at CNE. When she was on the radio with her two daily programs she continually pushed her listeners to be active in supporting the allied cause.

Kate was able to secure a scarf and helmet knitted by the two young princesses, Elizabeth and Margaret. Over one thousand dollars was raised in an auction at the Ex. This is comparable to at least forty or fifty thousand dollars today. Kate received a letter from the Queen's Lady in Waiting, stating how happy the Queen and the Princesses were that these two items had been used to raise this amount of money for relief in England.

The government called on Mrs. A to assist the Federal Wartimes Prices and Trade Board as its conservationism director. In an effort to get women to conserve and stretch scarce food and clothes supplies, the slogan for her campaign became, "Use it up, wear it out, make-over, make do."

The number of volunteer women's groups grew by leaps and bounds. By 1944, the volunteers in Canada had packed ten million packages for prisoners of war as well as sending multitudes of clothing, food, and books to both service people and civilians in war torn Britain.

Mrs. A was a leader in exhorting and teaching women. Her broadcasts gave advice on how to best use food in short supply, or what was the best food to substitute for a food that was not available. Her years of experience in preserving and canning garden products were continuously shared. An example of Kate's advice was how to save fats from meat so that it could be used for cooking in place of butter. The fat was to be placed in water, the water was to be boiled and then chilled. Strong tastes from the fat are left in the water. The fat is now close to tasteless.

Monday evening broadcasts were cooking schools that presented a week's menu. Close to four hundred women regularly attended this broadcast as a studio audience. As always, Kate found another purpose for these ladies while they were there. In her broadcasts Kate encouraged the listeners to send in all sorts of magazines that the family was finished with. She received thousands of magazines as well as other articles. The ladies at the Monday evening broadcast were asked to sort and package these articles. As in the times of the depression women at home looked forward to the daily broadcasts as Kate was a bright spot of the day breathing enthusiasm into the family atmosphere.

In the very middle of the war, Mrs. A toured Canada with her Remake revue. This tour had a wardrobe of remakes that was modeled by neighbourhood women. Kate travelled across Canada for six months. She visited all the major centers. Information was forwarded to each place to a group called Women's Voluntary Services. This group made the preparations. One of the preparations was to get three soldiers, three sailors, and three air force personnel. After the nine service men paraded out onto the stage, Kate would emphasize to her audience that here was the reason that cloth had to be conserved. It was needed for uniforms for the service people as well as to provide blankets, sheets, and bandages for their daily use.

It is estimated that Kate's appeals for overseas aid led to over a quarter of a million dollars' worth of clothing being sent to children's homes and maternity hospitals in England. Kate established a number of work rooms such as the space that Tamblyn's, one of her radio sponsors provided. As was the usual case, volunteer workers gathered to develop supplies from the materials and clothing that was received.

Kate loved to tell the story of a three year old boy who received a made over warm dressing gown. "One little boy, aged just three years, shell-shocked, completely alone in the world now: his voice lost in the terrible shock of an air raid…It took the rescue squad fourteen hours to dig out this little, stunned boy, and then he was taken from Manchester to an orphanage in Kent. One day, still silent since the terrible raid which killed his mother and daddy, the little tot was given his Remake dressing gown (which one of you listeners made) and he looked down at the colourful pattern on his Remake gown and his stunned eyes brightened. Suddenly he pointed at a particular pattern on his Remake gown and spoke for the first time. "My daddy wears socks like that, he said. And tears came to the eyes of the kindly matrons around the little soul."

Kate's father must have had as big a smile as this Irishman ever had as he looked down from his heavenly home and watched his daughter fight for Canada and the world through her efforts and leadership.

Chapter 21

The Incredible Mrs. A

In an article found in the CNE archives written by Nancy Kee, she says that Kate was the very essence of the perfect homemaker. She goes on to say that Mrs. A was bright, practical, and possessed a great sense of fun. The article's title is "The incredible Mrs. A."

With the approach to the opening of the yearly Ex, her hard working staff had to pick up the pace even to a greater level than they were already working. Last minute changes were a regular occurrence. Mrs. A eventually got a cot for her office. This was often her bed for the short night during the final days before the big show opened.

There were three restaurants run by the CNE. Kate had developed and ran all of them. The restaurants did all their own catering. Kate loved arranging the daily luncheons, which were held on the private balcony of the Women's Building. Over 200 guests from industry, big business and various professions were daily in attendance. The one exception was the Press, Radio, and TV luncheon when there were 600 guests. Mrs. A understood her calling.

This was an era when various contests were popular. Kate changed the contests yearly to meet the changing wishes of the people. Spelling bees, furniture made out of the orange crates of that day, hat trimming, typing contest, and candy were but a few offered. It was not that there were not problems. When the large Canadiana contest was held, the people were invited to send or bring their Canadiana to the Ex for judging. Each relic of Canadiana was to be returned to its rightful owner. However, the lady responsible for labeling the Canadiana took a casual approach. Many people ended up with the wrong item. Many others did not get their items back. After many weeks, many phone calls, and many visits of people to the Ex ground, the problems were solved to the satisfaction of the participants.

Just like the Beeton Fall Fair there was no area more fiercely competed in than the home baking section. One lady had won the butter tart competition for years. Then came the year when the prizes were being announced and she did not get the red ribbon. She also didn't get second place or third. She got no prize. She jumped to her feet, grabbed her tarts, and dumped the entire tray over the head of the chief judge. The stunned crowd watched the syrup, raisins, nuts, and pastry as it slid over his head down onto his clothes.

The following is an example of some of the days schedule during the Ex. These schedules were arranged by Kate.

Women's Building

Day by Day
<u>Standing Features</u>

12:00- 10:30	Princess Elizabeth wedding gown with attendants, East Wing
12:00- 10:30	Canadiana Exhibit, Alcove
10:00- 9:30	Handicrafts Exhibit, West Wing, Demonstrations of Weaving
10:00- 6:00	Handicrafts Exhibit, West Wing, Demonstrations of Canadian Guild of Potters
10:00- 9:30	Handicrafts Exhibit, West Wing, Demonstrations by the Metal Arts Guild
10:00- 9:30	Handicrafts Exhibit, West Wing, Demonstrations to be given by a Textile Block Printer
10:00- 9:30	Handicrafts Exhibit, West Wing, Demonstrations
10:00- 9:30	Handicrafts Exhibit, West Wing, Demonstrations to be given by a rug hooker

10:00- 9:30	Handicrafts Exhibit, West Wing, Demonstrations to be given by an Indian Basket Worker
12:00	Canadian Fashion Revue, Long Gallery
1:00	Canadian Fashion Revue, Long Gallery
1:00	High Style Fashion Show, Balcony Restaurant
2:00	Canadian Fashion Revue, Long Gallery
3:00	Canadian Fashion Revue, Long Gallery
3:30	High Style Fashion Show, Balcony Restaurant
4:00	Canadian Fashion Revue, Long Gallery
5:00	Canadian Fashion Revue, Long Gallery
6:00	Canadian Fashion Revue, Long Gallery
6:30	High Style Fashion Show, Balcony Restaurant
7:00	Canadian Fashion Revue, Long Gallery
8:00	Canadian Fashion Revue, Long Gallery
9:00	Canadian Fashion Revue, Long Gallery

Saturday August 28th (continued)

7:45	Career Women's Fashion Show
8:45	Songs to Remember
9:00	Tamblyn Broadcast
9:30	Hat Show

Monday August 30th – Children's Day

10:45	Jane Weston, CBL Commentator, Woman's World
11:15	June Dennis, CJBC Commentator, Woman's World
11:30	Marjorie Chadwick, CHUM Commentator, Woman's World
12:00	Music
12:30	The Craigs, CBL, Woman's World
1:00	Apron Competition, Woman's World Theatre, Coliseum
1:30	"Jack and Jill" Competition, Woman's World Theatre
2:00	Designers' Fashion Show
4:00	Hat Show
4:30	McCalls, Make It at Home

Here's Mrs. A.

5:00	Sing Song
7:00	McCalls, Make It at Home
7:30	Take off 10 pounds
7:45	Career Women's Fashion Show
8:15	Songs to Remember
9:00	Designers' Fashion Show
9:30	Hat Show

Tuesday August 31st - Automotive Day

10:45	Jane Weston, CBL Commentator, Woman's World
11:15	June Dennis, CJBC Commentator, Woman's World
11:30	Marjorie Chadwick, CHUM Commentator, Woman's World
12:00	Music
12:30	The Craigs, CBL, Woman's World
2:00	Designers' Fashion Show
2:30	Take Off 10 Pounds
2:45	Career Women's Fashion Show
3:15	Hat Show
3:45	McCalls, Make It at Home
4:15	Audience Sing Song
4:30	Designers' Fashion Show
5:00	Audience Sing Song
7:00	McCalls, Make It at Home
7:30	Take Off 10 Pounds
7:45	Career Women's Fashion Show
8:45	Songs to Remember
9:00	Tamblyn Broadcast
9:30	Hat Show

Chapter 22

A Proposed Music Program

There were always changes taking place in the programs. This is the nature of the CNE. A letter from Samuel Hersenhoren is suggesting a choir from Buffalo as a possible addition.

> Dear Mrs. Aitken:
> I wanted to tell you about this choir- picture attached. They are from Buffalo and it was over there that I heard about them. 100 children are in the active choir, with 50 more being trained as replacements. I have not heard them myself, but have the opinion of several professional musician friends there that the choir is simply wonderful! I have complete respect for their judgment, but wish that you and I could hear them sometime.
> The children wear red cassocks, with little white over-robes; they are of all denominations and are trained by a woman with apparently a great love of children, because there is a long waiting list of kiddies wanting to get in. They present all types of music- religious, secular, right down to the "Little Brown Bear Went Woof!" (Gets most audience applause).
> I didn't go into the matter further, except to acquire this picture which I must return to Buffalo. But it would be easy to get you more information, Mrs. Aitken, if you think that they would be a good draw for the Ex…either for the Sunday presentation or as a regular

daily feature. When I see you, I'd like to describe a couple of details about the choir that I cannot explain in writing- and, if you want, I can find out more about the organization.
    Sincerely,
    Samuel Hersenhoren

Mr. Hersenhoren also talked with Kate about the CNE centralizing the music program. The following are his recommendations.

Recommendation for Suggested Music Director Activities at CNE
1. It might be advisable to have one central focal point for the co-ordination of all music activities at the Ex. This would give the CNE authorities easy and complete control over these activities, as they would confer with and give instructions to just one man- who would thus be responsible for the performance and programming of music at the Ex.
2. This central bureau would help with the music competitions on every required way—selection of adjudicators, competitive pieces etc. In this regard, it might be a good idea to present an evening's concert "Music Winners of the EX" (a portion of which the C.B.C. might be persuaded to broadcast)—along the same lines as Kiwanis "Stars of the Festival".
3. Waltzes are always favorites, so my small string orchestra might present an hour of Waltzes every afternoon—perhaps during the tea hour on one of the pavilions. If space is available for a small dance-floor, there might be a "waltzing competition" one day—with judges from the local Arthur Murray dance studio.
4. "Parade of Bands" – a gala presentation of all the Toronto bands, plus the visiting band… as part of the celebration for Veteran's Day.
5. On Youth Day, various high-school bands (Toronto and out of town) could compete for a trophy—with the panel of judges to include the director of the visiting band, the head of the local Musicians Union etc.

6. On the evening of Radio day, a giant panorama of Canada's radio artists could be held—not just introduced to pull a number for a lucky draw, but to actually perform. Singers, comedians, instrumentalists, and orchestras- those whose names are well-known could be presented in a mammoth show, bound together by several successive masters-of-ceremonies. If this was a grand stand presentation, it should attract a large crowd.
7. Folk- Music Festival—choirs of different nationalities, in native costumes, singing their own songs... this could draw well, both their own people and those who are interested in the separate nationalities making up our Canada.
8. Miscellaneous ideas to be discussed- Barber Shop Quartet program, Jam Session (jazz) for the evening of youth day, and composers competition.

These are a few ideas which might prove interesting to CNE authorities—many more can be presented to fit in with each of the individual Days at the Ex. I would be happy to make more suggestions or discuss further the value of the central music co-ordination.

Chapter 23

A Script from a Radio Broadcast

The Tamblyn Drugstores were the prime sponsor of Kate's evening radio shows. The following is a partial script from a broadcast from the Ex in 1954.

Tamblyn Broadcast Wed. Sept.1, 1954

CY   What about the young lad you were telling us about who was an Exhibition visitor yesterday?

Aitken   On the way back our taxi driver, Earl Goodwin, was telling us about his 13 year old son Wayne. Yesterday was Wayne's day at the Ex. What a day! He and a couple of pals left the house at 8:30 in the morning and didn't get home until 10:30 last night. Wayne had saved up $5 of his own money and his dad matched it with another $5. So off he went and when he returned at night he brought back a giant sized jar of Lamorene and a pair of English cufflinks for his dad. He won both at the Ex. And young Wayne is a real shrewd young business man. He sold the Lamorene to his dad for $2.50 and is all set to go back to the Ex on Saturday.

CY   You mean he is not down there today?

Aitken   We asked his dad about that, and today is swimming day for Wayne. He is at the East York Kiwanis Tank today. And is his dad ever proud of him. "Wayne is a champion swimmer" he

	told us. In '53 and again in '54 he won in freestyle, the back stroke, and the breast stroke classes. Admission to the tank is 20 cents so Wayne packs a lunch and for his 20 cents gets a full day of swimming.
CY	Florence Chadwick better watch out or one of these years young Wayne is going to be stiff competition in the CNE swim. When is she swimming, Mrs. A?
Aitken	She starts between 9 o'clock and midnight on Monday and is expected to finish around supper time on Tuesday. Now into our telephone conversation. Rita could you get us Mrs.H.M. Metcalfe...Hudson 1-1232.

RING IN MRS. METCALFE- AD LIB TELEPHONE INTERVIEW WITH MRS. METCALFE

Aitken	We're mailing you a voucher for $5 worth of Tamblyn merchandise- you drop into your Willowdale store anytime on Friday and Mr. Wight will look after you.
CY	This is where I pick up the telephone- Rita could you get me Mrs. R. J. Smyth... Plymouth 5-2613 LINE BUSY unable to reach Mrs. Smith.
Aitken	Rita I'm calling Mrs. Shields- her number Plymouth 7-1438.

ADLIB TELEPHONE INTERVIEW WITH MRS.SHIELDS

Aitken	Your Tamblyn manager is Mr. Oakes and if you drop in any time Friday you can pick up your $5 worth of Tamblyn merchandise with all of our good wishes. Alright CY- pick up your phone.
CY	I'm calling Mrs. Harry Coughey at Walnut 3-1039- could you get me that number please Rita?

ADLIB CONVERSATION WITH MR. COUGHEY (bachelor)

Here's Mrs. A.

CY — Well I'd advise you – as well as some film to pick up one of the new cook books in Tamblyn's- you'll get a lot of bright ideas out of that. Thank you sir, good night.

Aitken — Well that's the calls for tonight, I hope you've enjoyed it as much as we have- don't forget that the homemade pickles…

CY — with recipes in the new Cook Book…

Aitken — Are on view at ten Tamblyn stores this week- after you're through looking at them, they go to Queen Elizabeth Hospital for the immobilized patients there.

CY — We have a baby!

Aitken — Whose? Yours? Horace's? C.F.R.B's?

CY — No- It's the JOHNSON & JOHNSON baby- and TAMBLYN baby.

Aitken — And a lucky baby he is—he's today's winner of the JOHNSON AND JOHNSON BABYLAND BOX from TAMBLYN'S. You know one is given away daily to a new baby born during the previous week.

CY — The proud parents of tonight's baby are Mr. And Mrs. Stephen Myshawada of 149 Park Road in South Oshawa.

Aitken — They still haven't got the young gentleman named- but he was born last Friday and weighed 7lbs 1oz

CY — And Mrs. Myshawada should that young son of yours cry, it might be because of prickly heat rash. That's where the JOHNSON'S baby powder in this gift comes in- it soothes baby's skin fast… keeps him happy and fresh during hot weather. The rest of you mothers, buy a tin of JOHNSON'S baby powder today at TAMBLYN'S. Save with the big economy size tin at the new low price—just 59 cents.

Horace — //////////////////////////

CY — This is Cy Strange signing off your TAMBLYN broadcast off the air. We'll be back tomorrow night, same time, same station, same folks. That's a date.

Chapter 24

And The Beat Goes On

There are those who have said Kate Aitken was Canada's Martha Stewart. The only area that the two might be compared has to be in cooking and possibly some general household hints. As has already been illustrated, Mrs. A really was Canada's woman of the 20th century.

By the time the war was over, she was a household name. She was a big time radio broadcaster, and radio was where it was at. When Kate travelled about the country, people wanted to see her and meet her. She was Canada's best known woman. It was estimated that one of every three people in Canada listened to one or the other broadcasts. When women were at CNE, they often waited to catch a glimpse of Mrs. A. When she did appear she was always perfectly groomed. For several years she was on the list of Canada's ten best dressed women.

In the early 1950's she was being given titles like the World's Busiest Woman. The Toronto Star Weekly had an article calling Mrs. A, Canada's Chatter Queen. This was not an insult, at the time she had twenty-one secretaries. Her daughters, their husbands, even grandchildren and friends were often called upon to assist in her work. Kate assumed that they would help when needed. And they were needed.

Mrs. A received as many as 260,000 pieces of mail a year and spoke up to one hundred and fifty times during that year. By the mid 1950's, Kate estimated that she had been a speaker for over four thousand occasions.

Here's Mrs. A.

Mrs. A was at the front of the line in observing and being part of the changing role of women. This was not an issue. It was part of who she was. It is not Canadian to be radical. It is Canadian to change when change is required. And times were changing.

After being a major part of the work force during World War I, women were encouraged after the war to drop out of the workforce. The Depression years only led to reinforcing this idea. World War II would be a major catalyst to change the women's role forever. During the years of WWII the number of women in the work force doubled from six hundred thousand to one million two hundred thousand. It became respectable for women to work outside of the home and work beyond domestic roles.

When the war was in its third year, the women's branches of the armed forces began to emerge. By the end of the war over forty five thousand women were part of the Canadian Armed Forces. Just under four hundred of these received military decorations.

Kate was not a war correspondent but she made a number of plane trips to England in order to bring back to her listening audience a firsthand report of what was going on over on the other side of the ocean. Because her nature was to be always positive, Mrs. A was an encouragement to the women of Canada, - just like Winston Churchill was always positive in his leadership of the free world.

In the early time of the war, her daughter Anne entered the teaching profession and daughter Mary worked in a factory that was supporting the war effort. Mary was never far from her mother's side to give the help and support that Mrs. A required. Mary was like her mother's assistant, but by personal choice, usually in the background.

Chapter 25

Total Organization

A major ingredient in Kate's life was her ability to organize every activity that she was involved with.

In the early 1920s while she was developing her delivery business in Toronto, she developed a set of standards for quality control for her products. She made this list so that she could advise country women who were good cooks as to how they could stay at home, develop a delivery system to Toronto and earn extra money while looking after their children. The following were Kate's quality control recommendations.

In setting prices, allow for containers. Nowadays plastic or waxed cartons are inexpensive and suited to every need, but that costs should not be omitted.

Don't discount the cost of attractive wrapping materials. In a year's operation you'll use plenty. If your bank balance will stand the strain, buy six months' supply at a time.

Cakes light as a feather and covered with frothy icing don't journey well. Pound cakes, spice cakes or light fruit cakes, with either a dusting of icing sugar or a good solid icing, can come out of a collision or sharp turn as good as new.

Rich cookies crumble in transit. Hermits, oatmeal cookies or gingersnaps travel well. Use the same size cookie cutters all the time; set your price by weight and not by count, since the cookie batter sometimes rolls more thinly than at others. Buy broken nutmeats, which are a great deal cheaper than the whole variety.

Always draw the chickens and thoroughly cleanse and chill heart, liver, gizzard and neck; wrap in wax paper and tuck inside the bird. When delivering take a moment to show your customer how she can button-hole the incision made for dressings, which saves her sewing up the bird after stuffing. The method is simple. With a sharp paring knife make one inch slits in the end projections of the bird. This makes a neat and easy closing.

Never, never stuff the bird before delivery. If dressing is requested, package it separately. Leave roasting instructions with each bird so that it isn't ruined in a too hot oven.

Never wash the eggs, since this removes the coating which helps to keep them fresh. If any mark needs to be removed, use steel wool. Grade the eggs carefully so that they're either extra large, large, medium or pullets. Nothing upsets a customer so much as an uneven grading. She thinks they should all be as big as the biggest. A special treat for the children is the colored Easter eggs, easily done with vegetable coloring.

Pack the unsalted butter in brown earthenware pots rather than making it up in pound prints. I had a little wooden stamp made with a flower design which, pressed on top of the bowl of butter, gave it a fresh from the farm look. Warn your customers that fresh butter does not keep as well as salted butter. Only one week's supply should be ordered at a time and it should be kept well refrigerated.

Never sell cream unless you have the facilities to keep it chilled during transport.

Pies, to taste really homemade, should not be lifted from the pie pan, and it's only in a proper pie pan that the bottom crust is cooked to perfection. Therefore in charting your costs add the cost of this container, which is refunded on the return of the original pie pan. You'll notice I said "original". Keep to a standard 9" deep pie pan, or even with the most honest customer you'll find yourself loaded with shallow 7" pans, which are no good for fruit pies. All our pie pans have initialed square of adhesive tape on bottom.

Homemade bread should be regulation size, so that sliced it fits into the toaster. Before the bread dough is shaped for the pan, weigh it to keep it standard. Rolls should be made a dozen to a pan so that the size and weight are uniform.

Before packing jams and jellies, inspect each jar carefully to see whether or not any moisture has seeped through at the sides. If so, lift off wax and reheat in an earthenware pitcher placed in boiling water. Now with tissue blot up the moisture. Then re-apply the coating of hot wax.

Because such work is highly individual, every little gimmick you can add brings return far beyond the money or time expended. In the autumn we always tucked in a few colored maple leaves. For Christmas the hamper was topped with green boughs. Labels for the jams, jellies or pickles were always hand printed and signed.

Chapter 26
Travel Alone and Love It

It was in the early 1920's that Kate had begun to travel for the Department of Agriculture. This was the beginning of a life of travelling not only in Canada but the entire world.

Her early experiences were centered in Canada. She travelled with other team members-all male except for her, on their visits to well-to-do farm communities as well as very poorly farmed communities. The size of team varied but was usually four or five members. No day was ever exactly the same as another. There were days that they had to fight to hold the attention of the people. These were groups who knew the agricultural field much better than the team members. Kate learned the significance of the advice once given by Franklin D Roosevelt, "Be brief, be sincere, be seated."

One of the winter trips took her to Manitoulin Island. The team went by rail to Little Current. As the connecting lake was frozen over, they travelled by sleigh over to the island. The sleigh had a canvas top with the only visible part of the people in the sleigh being the drivers' fur-covered head and the mittens on his hands. Inside the canvas was a cool burning stove, a lantern, a table, some chairs and a deck of cards.

In this igloo on a sleigh, Kate and her companions played euchre to pass the time of the hour trip.

Kate's' transportation on one of her summer trips was the local mail carrier who knew everyone in the area. He not only delivered the mail but he also ran errands for the people on the mail route. He took things that needed to go to town from the people on the route and he brought things back from the town. On this day he had round steak, baking powder, shoe laces and buttons. When Kate asked him if he got paid for making these deliveries, he was quick to reply that he would not be taking money from his friends and neighbors. On the other hand these same friends and neighbors would not take advantage of him. He often received pies and tarts as well as roasting chicken or even a duck. The storekeeper gives him little treats or even bigger treats for things that he picks up for him.

On another occasion Kate arrived at a small hamlet on her schedule, only to discover that everything in the hamlet was closed down because of an epidemic of measles. There were three women waiting for Kate to assist her with the classes. They were wondering what they could do. Kate said that they could make tea biscuits. She went on to say that she had often thought that there were enough different kinds of biscuits so that there could be a different tea biscuit for every week of the year. A lost day was turned into an exciting time as the four of them eagerly experimented with all the ingredients that they could find to make different kinds of biscuits. This day led to a very successful cookbook entitled "52 Kinds of Tea Biscuits".

Will Rodgers once said, "People change but not much". There was the night that Kate's group was in the same town as three livestock inspectors. The six government officials met for dinner. The main subject at the dinner table was shop talk. Each person was sharing some of the fun happenings that they had experienced on the road. They were having a very enjoyable time when a big red faced man at the next table said in a very loud voice that he had been talking with a neighbor's friend, Jimmy Jones, who was well set up. Another man at the table said that he thought Jimmy was sick. The red faced man replied that he had been sick with a problem with his brain but he had gone to his Doctor and the Doctor told Jimmy to leave his brains with him for a week. He would clean them. Jimmy left his brains with the Doctor but never came back. The Doctor met him on the street and mentioned to him that he hadn't come back and wondered why Jimmy said that he didn't need them. He said that he had gotten a government job.

Chapter 27

World Travel

When Kate made her trip to England for the British Empire craft show in 1928, it was the beginning of her world travels that would continue for more than three decades.

A farm journal had financed a continuing trip to Scotland, Ireland, Holland, Denmark, Belgium and France.

Kate was full of anticipation as she went first to Ireland and then to Scotland. Because of the Irish background of her Father and the Scottish background of Ann Scott's mother, Kate had heard many romantic stories of both lands. She was not disappointed.

When she arrived at the village inn near the farm in Donegal County where the Scotts lived, the innkeeper had a room already for her. He took her up the narrow stairs to a small bedroom. When he turned down the covers, he discovered that the bed was damp. He told Kate that she would need a night cap. Kate had a vision of nice hot totty. The nightcap turned out to be a knitted woolen head dress that fitted snuggly over her head and tucked into her nightgown. A chuckling Kate slipped into her feather bed to enjoy a good night's sleep before journeying early the next day to the farm.

Kate visited with neighbors of her relatives who were leaders in the Wyandotte's chicken business in Ireland.

When she journeyed on to Scotland, she visited an experimental farm that had prize poultry.

The highlight of her visit to Scotland was visiting the St Giles Church in Edinburgh. It brought life to her grandmothers' description of Scotland and this church. John Knox, the founder of the Presbyterian Church, is buried just outside St Giles on Parliament Square. A flat tablet set in the pavement marks his grave. Kate experienced the high pulpit, the great choir loft and the dim light as her grandmother had described it.

Kate returned to the church for an evening service where the minister was preaching to the student body of Edinburgh University. The sermon was pure fire, hell and damnation. The minister reminded the congregation that there was a beautiful heaven waiting for those who lived their lives by the lessons taught by the Shorter Catechism.

In bed that night, Kate set aside her other reading as she recalled the Shorter Catechism that her Father had taught her three decades earlier in her young life.

It was in Denmark that Kate learned the meaning of farm economy. A farm of thirty acres was considered to be a large holding. Every last inch of it was cultivated. There was no room for fences and no place for a head land. The fields were plowed roughly to the road and the boundary with a neighbor was marked by a stake.

Evening agriculture classes were held to encourage intelligent farming. Both the husband and wife attended these classes as the farm business was considered to be a partnership. The farm was owned jointly by the married couple.

Kate flew from Denmark to Holland. This was still the early days of aviation. Kate would never forget this flight. Almost every person on board was sick. This plane had no bags to assist the sick and there was only one washroom.

In Holland, Kate was once more impressed by the thrift and the cleanliness of the entire farm operation. Conservation was already an important word to these farmers.

When Kate arrived home in Toronto after a long and rough Atlantic flight she went to give her final copy of her trip to her editor.

The editor told Kate that the earlier copy she had sent was not well received by the Canadian farmers. They did not appreciate being criticized.

Kate's response was typical. Kate said "she was not the least bit upset by the editor's comments." She told him that he had sent her to report what she saw. She had done exactly that.

The drive from Toronto to Beeton ended with a joyous reunion over supper with Henry, Anne and Mary.

There is no place like home.

Chapter 28

The Royal Family

This entire book could be devoted to the travels of Mrs. A. Her adventures and escapades were many.

It seemed that anytime that there was a big event with the Royal Family, Kate was inevitably present. The wedding of Elizabeth and Phillip had the eyes of the entire British Empire and the western world focused on London, Buckingham Palace and Westminster Abbey.

On the night before the wedding the streets around the palace and the streets that lead to the Abbey were crowded with people who never went to bed that night. The people were too excited to go to sleep. Besides, they wanted a ringside location to view the events of the next day.

Kate recalls the last view of Phillip and Elizabeth before they retired for the night. The soft woodland green of the dress worn by the Princess, the gleam of the engagement ring on her finger, the gentle way she laid her arm on Phillips' etched in Mrs. A's memory; two young people very much in love.

An amusing event that happened in the Abbey was when World War II hero, Winston Churchill, arrived. He was no longer Prime Minister as he had been defeated in the last election by Clement Attlee's Labor Party. He was now the leader of the opposition.

Mr. Churchill was greeted with applause. Flushed and smiling he walked to the section reserved for the Commonwealth Prime Ministers. The seated Prime Ministers also applauded the war hero. Instinct led him to turn to the right when he came to the end of the aisle-the front row of Prime Ministers. He almost sat on Prime Minister Clement Attlee's knee. The entire Prime ministers' section broke into laughter. In typical Churchill style, he smiled, bowed to Mr. Attlee and took his seat on the left side.

When the service was over, Kate headed for the BBC headquarters where she was making her broadcasts. She didn't wait for the elevators but took the steps three at a time down to the studio three floors below ground level.

The BBC staff quickly gave her a heavily sugared cup of hot tea while she caught her breath and organized her notes.

She had a half an hour of time in which she made six five minute segments to be sent back to Canada to her eagerly waiting audiences. Television was still in the future for rural Canada. Instantaneous relays of information were only in their infancy stage.

Mrs. A's reports would be amongst the first information to reach Canada. The Royal couple came on an extended tour of Canada and the United States in 1951. The twenty five year old princess left an ailing royal father at home. Elizabeth always was willing to assume responsibility even as a young girl during the war years. She was not in the background. She was front and centre. When the tour was ending, Mrs. A reported that the slender young shoulders of the Princess appeared to bear too heavy a burden. One can't help but wonder what Mrs. A would report today after this Princess has now celebrated sixty years as the Queen.

Kate found during this long trip that it was a nerve-racking struggle to turn out a different story every day about the royal family. Mrs. A thought the smartest female writer of this time was a lady with the American Press. This reporter stayed in her hotel room to listen to all of the broadcasts of the day on her radio. After hearing all of the broadcasts she wrote her story. She was never fighting with crowds, nor was she ever cold, wet or tired. From her hotel room she wrote, according to Mrs. A, some of the most amazing eyewitness reports that could possibly be produced. This reporter received an increase in pay when she returned home after the tour.

The following is Mrs. A's description of her trip to Elizabeth's coronation in 1952.

The coronation necessitated the most intensive advance planning. Hotel accommodation had to be laid on, passes arranged for, and transport assured. Most important of all, the details of the five –hour ceremonial had to be so familiar that the broadcast would flow without any slip-ups.

On the overnight transatlantic light, I reviewed the order of service, inch by inch. Since this was an occasion which would not be repeated and since these broadcasts were tremendously important, I didn't sleep as well as usual. But when we arrived at London airport the feeling of excitement was contagious.

Planes were landing from all parts of the world. As each foreign delegation arrived, the flag of its country was run up the flagpoles along the airstrip. Here were color, pageantry and a babble of foreign voices 'Look'" someone would say, "there's the party from India", or "The Australians have landed", or "Here come the representatives from the Gold Coast."

As we drove up to the city every row of flats, every tiny shop, every restaurant, every industrial plant was flag-bedecked. Barely taking time to check into my hotel, I went sight-seeing. Almost overnight, London had become a floral city. The streets leading to the palace were overhung with great golden baskets in which bloomed every English flower. Bond Street, Piccadilly, Regent Street, Birdcage Walk, all had conforming decorations, a symphony of color. More touching still were the tiny window boxes, beloved of Londoners, installed on every ledge and blooming bravely.

Everywhere in London was the sound of hammering and the smell of fresh paint. Stands along the route were being finished by the carpenters; as the last nail was driven, the painters moved in. Uneasy shop-owners were fitting wooden barricades in front of plate-glass windows and road barriers were being set up. As if by magic, arrows designating the line of the processional were being erected, and the color-film merchants were doing a land office business.

My sponsors had asked me to fly over three days in advance of the coronation, so that I could not only beam back broadcasts but also take pictures of the pre-coronation activities. Saturday, Sunday and Monday I toured the city in a cab, shooting pictures from the tops of monuments, inside restaurants, and from the back seat of the taxi. To expedite the arrival of the film in Canada, a courier called at the hotel every afternoon at five o'clock to pick up the day's take and deliver it to the airport.

This lad, a former member of the London Metropolitan Police, could get through traffic like an eel; he seemed the logical answer to the problem of transport on the day of the coronation. Not only did I have to get to the Abbey in time for the ceremony, but had to take advance pictures of the crowds, the arrival of celebrities, and portions of the procession. With the consent of Scotland Yard, my official car pass was placed on the courier's motorcycle; and a side car was added which would accommodate not only the camera and myself but also my coronation outfit, carefully packed in a box.

Our Canadian pre-coronation dinner ended at 2 A.M. Three hours later, at five o'clock, the courier and I were on our way. We went first to Kensington where the military bands were quartered, then broke for breakfast. Trafalgar Square, a strategic point of the procession, was our next objective and a very happy one. British crowds, always co-operative, offered us every assistance. Seeing the poised camera, two sturdy workmen said, "we'll hoist you up miss and you'll get a real good view."

By mid morning a misty drizzle had turned into a downpour. Although it did not dampen the spirits of spectators, it did cut off the view. Lords and ladies en route to the Abbey hastily had the chauffer run up the car top. But six=foot-three Queen Salote of Tonga was impervious to the weather (it always rains in Tonga). In her full regalia of red robes and a feathered headdress she beamed, waved, and mopped rain from her face. Cheers followed every foot of her progress to the Abbey.

By this time both the courier and I were soaked to the skin, but we had our pictures. Before leaving for the airport with the film, he delivered me to one of the rear entrances of the Abbey. Luck was with me; a word from him and I was allowed to change into my coronation outfit in a small backroom. Through the kindness of friends my seat was in the section set aside for Lesser Nobility.

The coronation ceremony is as old as England and as impressive as history. But the memory that remained with me was the look of dedication on the face of the young monarch. I had seen her in every phase of her life-as a child just learning to walk, as a young A.T.S. recruit, as a radiant bride, as a charming ambassador for her country. But on this coronation day the soft, youthful roundness of the face was gone, character had emerged. From where I sat and as the ceremony proceeded, noticeable was the gradual paling of the face and the tiny lines of strain. The heavy gold vestments of office, the crown, and the responsibilities of state seemed a heavy burden for a young queen. But leaving the Abbey we were all convinced that here was a royal strength.

Chapter 29
The Hungarian Revolution, 1956

When Kate was asked if her work at the Canadian National Exhibition had resulted in much financial reward, Kate's response was that she gained very little. She went on to say that a major weakness of hers was always that the success of the job was much more significant than any financial reward.

Her work in reporting the Hungarian Revolution shows the amazing depth of this lady's character. Her own words give it a vivid description.

Rome, Madrid, London, Paris, Berlin-these and other places I have seen both before and after the devastation of war. But most poignant and heart breaking was the Austrian-Hungarian border following the ill-fated October revolution in 1956.

A month after the initial uprising, I flew to Vienna to report on the actual conditions of the Hungarian refugees and the help needed. Arriving in the city at twelve noon, at 12:30 we started our survey of the refugee hostels situated within the city. Empty houses, unused buildings and abandoned castle were all in use. Vienna, the home of the beautiful women and Strauss waltzes, only lately released from Russian domination, had overnight become a city of mercy. At five o'clock each evening a voluntary exodus from the city took place. By devious routes, cars, station wagons and trucks moved from the city to take up their vigil on the border. Throughout the long night these volunteers picked up the escapees and rushed them either to the first-aid hospitals behind the line or to the transit camps scattered throughout the countryside.

My multi-lingual driver knew every back road leading to the border. When we arrived at the point of watch the car was blacked out and left in a getaway position. At the edge of the marsh that separates Austria and Hungary we stood waiting for the rustle in the grass which means an escaping refugee. No word was spoken, no cigarette was lit. The minutes seemed endless.

Then came the sound for which we had been waiting. Said Franz, "Someone is crawling through the marsh." In tense silence, we strained eyes and ears. After what seemed an eternity the figure of a man on hands and knees did emerge. We picked him up, desperate, wounded, almost unconscious from loss of blood. Crossing the border, this twenty seven year old Hungarian had been shot in the knee but had managed to crawl to safety. We rushed him to the first-aid post where doctors and nurses waited for just such emergencies.

Later that night we picked up a little three year old whose mother had previously escaped to Vienna. Smuggled to the border by an elderly neighbor, the child had her mothers' name and address, written on pieces of cotton sewn to her garments.

But most devastating of all were two boys, eleven and fourteen, whose parents had maneuvered their escape. You might wonder why any parent would willingly part with children. One method to crush the revolution was this: if parents in Hungary were suspected, sons between the ages of twelve and twenty, and daughters from fourteen to twenty-two, could be seized and deported to labor camps. Frantic parents felt that even the uncertainty of escape by the children was preferable to the risk of deportation.

When the boys came whimpering over the bank like animals, they were incoherent. Rushed to the first-aid station, they were given a sedative. When we called back to enquire about them, the doctor said, "Hiding under a bush just on the border, they were flushed out by a guard. It was either kill or be killed. They choked him to death." Haunted by this story, I asked the doctor, "Will they ever forget this experience?"

He paused briefly, looked out the window. "I don't know," he said, "but what you North Americans must remember is that these children have grown up in a police state where there is no security for happiness or normal living."

Security...happiness...normal living. How must it feel to walk out of your home and close the door behind you, leaving forever the familiar sights and sounds , the table at which you ate, the clothes you had worn, the garden you had tended; leaving the radio turned up, so that neither police nor neighbors suspect that you were striking off into the darkness and an unknown future.

Chapter 30

Closer to Home

One of the letters that Kate read over the air in the early years of her broadcast was a letter from a grandmother whose son was on relief. It was in the heart of the depression. The grandmother stated the family had absolutely no money for Christmas presents. Her small granddaughter had sent a number of letters to Santa Claus asking for a doll. The grandmother's letter was asking if anyone could give a doll. The listeners' response was not only many dolls but doll clothes and carriages. A number of young girls received dolls that Christmas from Mrs. .A's Santa Clauses.

The thank you broadcast that followed was heard by an eleven year old girl who was at home because she was sick. She wrote a letter saying how great it was that the little girl had got her doll. She went on to say that she was too big to play with dolls but she really could use a piano. Mrs. A wrote a note in which she said to this eleven year old that she did not know how a piano could be delivered to the girl's home. This young eleven year old replied with another letter stating that it would be no problem to get the piano because her Dad drove his truck to Toronto every week. She went on to say that it would be so great to get the piano because a Sunday school was beginning in her family home. Mrs. A was at a service club luncheon shortly after this. She mentioned to an acquaintance about the piano request. Without hesitation he said that their family had a piano that they were no longer using.

The piano was tuned up and packed into the Father's truck.

To help the little girl learn how to play the piano, a book of easy instructions were included. The new Sunday school opened on the Queen Victoria Holiday weekend. After the first Sunday, the eleven year old again wrote to Mrs. A. She said that she had played "Jesus Loves Me" and "Onward Christian Soldiers". She played "Jesus Loves Me" with two hands but only used one hand with Onward Christians Soldier". She said that the bass notes were hard for her to read.

Chapter 31

Home

It was early October, in 1954. There had been a lot of rain that fall. On this Friday morning, the rain began early and continued as a downpour throughout the day. The Beetonia Hotel closed at 5:30 for the dinner hour. It was the law of the Province of Ontario that beverage rooms were to close at supper time.

One group of five people left from the hotel and headed east on the eighth line to Bond Head and Newton Robinson. It was only a half an hour after the hotel closed that water was running in the back windows of the hotel basement and was running out the front windows. This was just inches below the first floor.

The five travelers moved along the eighth line until they came to Wilcox Creek. Wilcox Creek was ordinarily little more than a stream that a person could step over. On this Friday evening the tide was flowing rapidly over the top of the bridge. The car stalled on the bridge. The five passengers scrambled to the roof of the car. Help came. The municipal road maintainer (grader) was driven out into the water upstream from the car as far as the operator would dare go. A boat was attached to a rope and floated down stream to the car. It worked. The five people were moved from the roof of the car to the boat. As the last person got off the car into the boat, the car turned on its side, hit the boat and all five people were thrown into the water where they all drowned.

It was sometime in the early evening that Irwin Joyce, a popular young member of Mrs. A's; St Andrew Church was coming home from Toronto. Unaware of the raging creek, he drove into it. His young bright light would not shine anymore except in the memory of the young people he had influenced.

The Holland Marsh is less than half an hours' drive from Beeton. For a number of years a three ton truck from the Marsh would be at the main corner in Beeton at 6:30 A.M. on a Saturday morning. Teenagers from the village would load into the back of the truck to go and pick weeds, or vegetables for the day. The pay varied according to the observation of the supervisor.

The slower workers, usually the smaller teens got $.25 an hour and the fastest workers made $.50 an hour. At the end of the day, the same truck took the tired teens back to Beeton. On this Friday night of Hurricane Hazel, the area of the Holland Marsh was completely devastated by the roaring water that covered the ground. One large family spent the night in their home which had broken away from its foundation. The home became a boat. The family kept afloat by running from one side of the house to the other.

When the side that they were on began to sink, they would run to the other side. When the morning arrived and the raging water had subsided, the family and their ravaged home were safe on the ground.

Most families from the Marsh had been evacuated to Bradford, where feeding centers were established and trailer camps were set up.

Mrs. A continually monitored the Holland Marsh story on her broadcasts. Her listeners provided blankets, clothing and food for the people who were originally from the Netherland, Belgium, Italy, Poland and Germany.

As Christmas approached, the listeners provided toys as well as turkeys. Mrs. A decided to produce a remote broadcast at the trailer camp in the Holland Marsh to help bring the people of the Marsh and Mrs. A's listeners together. The broadcast consisted of Christmas Carols sang by the various national groups in their native languages.

The closing song on the broadcast was 'Now thank we all our God, with heart and hands and voices, who wondrous things have done,in whom his world rejoices' It was sung by the German children.

Kate found it difficult to sign off the broad cast without a break in her voice.

As Mrs. A travelled home that evening with her broadcast team of two others, the car was quiet. As they neared Toronto, the program announcer said" You know, there are two kinds of courage, the courage in battle and the courage to face the long, hard pull. It's the second kind we have seen tonight."

Chapter 32

The End of an Era

When Mrs. A retired from her regular radio broadcasts in June of 1957, Lloyd Lockhart wrote in the Toronto Star Weekly magazine "Kate Aitken-after twenty four years of fabulous activity, is more than a personality, she's an institution. She got to the top by doling out words of hope and encouragement to all, and give her credit-the party line that she is now dissolving stretches from coast to coast and reaches at least one and a half million listeners on a daily basis. There has never been anything like it as witnessed by her fan mail of 350,000 letters a year."

The question that was asked was why was she retiring? She was a very healthy sixty five years old who continued to show an abundance of energy. Kate's response to the question was that she had always been unpredictable. She went on to say that she had always tried to do what was right. In this case, retirement from her radio broadcasts was what was right.

As Mrs. A's life is studied it becomes more and more obvious that she always had a sixth sense to be on the cutting edge. Her ability to be in the right place at the right time, to be involved in some project when her involvement would be significant and to move on to a new happening when her work was finished was always an outstanding part of Mrs. A.

The 30s, 40s and 50s were the high point of the radio as a communication link in Canada. The radio presented the most recent news and weather. It was family entertainment. It was the major link of the mostly rural Canada to other people and a world that was often very remote.

By the late 1950s, this was changing. The Canadian society was becoming less rural. City-centered living was rapidly increasing. Automobile travel was continuing to accelerate. People were beginning to travel to "exotic" places for vacations. Florida was not just a place where wealthy people vacationed.

More and more women were entering the work force. Younger women in particular were at their place of work and didn't have time to attend afternoon meetings. The Women's Institute was losing its significance.

And then there was television. In the late 50s this new beacon of communication was entering rural Ontario as the new source of entertainment. Foster Hewitt and Hockey Night in Canada could now be seen, even if the screen was often very snowy, Saturday night wrestling with Whipper Billy Watson and Yukon Eric became a family staple. Snack foods like popcorn and potato chips began to replace homemade food.

When CFRB began looking for a replacement for Mrs. A, the station interviewed over two hundred women for the job. No one was hired. It seemed like the station was not sure what qualities they were looking for.

Eventually, Betty Kennedy was hired. When she appeared on the scene the interviewers knew that she was not Kate Aitken. They also knew that they liked what they saw and heard.

Mrs. A had been dubbed by her CFRB co-host Gordon Sinclair as the busiest woman in the world. She was a feminine dynamo who shared each of her experiences with her audience who loved her for what she was. She was not interested in pushing any social cause. Mrs. A believed in hard work, perseverance, individual initiative, and giving help to improve the world of Canada.

Chapter 33

Always a Writer

During Mrs. A's years on the radio, she always wrote her own script. She often wrote over nine thousand words in a day. It was not unusual for this daily script to be rewritten as many as four times in order for the words to be just exactly what Mrs. A wanted to say.

Writing had always been part of her life going back to the days in her Father's store when Robert Scott would get her to write the ad for the store's weekly specials. Kate's father had noticed on his daughter's school reports that her English composition marks were exceptional.

He, himself, did not want to take the time to prepare the ad. On the other hand' Kate's father was seldom satisfied with her first effort. Like daughter like father, Mr. Scott would have Kate rework the ad until he was satisfied. Interestingly, it often took four attempts by the daughter before the father was satisfied.

Young Kate's reputation in the Beeton community as a writer soon became well known. She was asked to write farewell addresses for teachers and ministers who were moving on to a new town and a new experience. Mrs. A continually showed her ability to be positive.

For the departing teacher she would write "Although it is with great reluctance that we say good-bye to you, the memory of the precepts that you have instilled in us will always remain as a steadying influence in this community." For the departing clergyman, she wrote "In any future charge we know that you will give the same inspiration to the young, the same gentle consideration to the sick, and comfort to the dying. Our loss will be Stroud's gain."

Young brides and grooms sought her assistance. Kate would write for them "Two young people embarking on the sea of matrimony, all good wishes for a smooth, happy voyage. May all your troubles be little ones."

Mrs. A's fascination with words continued to grow. When she went to the teachers' courses, the library at the school had a steady visitor. The librarian, the schools' English master, asked her to come into his office. He asked the young lady if she read all of the books that she checked out. She assured him that she did. He asked her why she read all that she did. Her response was that she would like to write a book herself.

The master responded with words Kate never forgot. He said that everyone would like to write a book. Young people like her had plenty of ideas. However, it was a long process to put these ideas on paper. His suggestion to Kate was to forget about writing a book until she learned to think and how to express these thoughts.

During the next forty years of her life Mrs. A would continuously be writing, whether it was for a magazine article, for her radio show, or for a presentation that she was to make. It was not until the 1950s that this very busy woman began to seriously write books, although she had a number of cookbooks available to the public at least a decade before.

Chapter 34
The Process of Writing

Here is Mrs. A's own description of the thought processes that went into all of her writing of magazine articles and especially of booklets and books on cooking.

If you have the desire to put words on paper, don't let anyone discourage you. But by the same token, don't try to write about something you've never experienced or places that you've never visited. As Women's Editor of a weekly magazine, my work included food, fashions, human interest stories, the care and rearing of children, interior decoration, new trends in home making, advice to the lovelorn. This assignment came after I had struggled through young love, marriage, children, meals, clothes, painting and wallpapering a home, and trimming my own hats.

The vocabulary for each type of story is different, so first learn the vernacular. That means constant research, intelligent listening, and a feeling for the background. Once you've accomplished this, the phrases, the expressions are as comfortable and well-fitting as an outfit you love and in which you feel completely at home.

What is the most difficult copy to write? Definitely the most time-consuming and the most exacting is food copy. What you write is being read by women who've been preparing meals, or who expect to prepare them, all their lives. If, having tried your recipe, a reader is unsuccessful, you've lost a friend who will never trust you again. Food is too expensive to throw away. But as well as careful directions, women like variations on the main theme. I've always maintained that women don't get bored with cooking, but rather with making the same dish over and over again. So, even in the plainest recipe, it's essential to toss in a new slant, a different spice, or a different method of serving.

Hung in our test kitchen are own Ten Commandments for efficiency:

Never publish a recipe that hasn't been tested at least three times. This triplicate testing establishes beyond doubt the ingredients, the oven temperature, and the finished product.

Always use standard-size pans and utensils. To help the young bride, include a line like "Bake in a loaf pan 9"x 5"x 3"," or "Bake in a two-quart casserole dish," or "Pour batter, we follow a recipe with a short footnote that says, "This batter is thin," or "This batter is quite heavy." This directive relieves her mind and, it could be, saves putting a flop before the young bride-groom.

Don't get so carried away that recipes include such exotic items as button mushrooms, ground hazel nuts, or cardamom seeds. Not only are they expensive but often not available.

Specify the kind of flour used. There are three general kinds-pastry, all purpose, and cake flour. They all react differently.

Sugar should be similarly designated-white sugar, brown sugar, icing sugar, or fruit sugar.

Follow the food trends. Ready mixes, frozen foods, and ready-cut meats have altered food preparation to a remarkable degree.

Be precise with recipes. Ingredients should be arranged in the order of mixing. For easier mixing each separate movement should be in a sentence by itself.

Always include number of servings, or yield of cookies, hot biscuits or muffins.

With the meat recipes include a chart that shows the name of every cut and where located.

In reading cook-book copy, don't stay with it too continuously or table spoons will be confused with teaspoons. Without doubt it is the hardest copy in the world to check.

Words for cookbook copy- this Is where the vernacular comes in. A cake should be moist, tender, delectable, light as a feather. A salad is appetizing, intriguing, attractive or crisp. Pastry should be flaky, puffy, golden-brown or rich. Gravy should be velvet-smooth and brown. Stewed occasionally through the copy can be such words as embellish, festive, pungent and titillating-but not too often.

There is something tremendously gratifying is compiling a cookbook. A well tested one takes at least a year. But if it is well tested you know that it will stay there in the kitchen, be used day after day, and become a family friend. The pages on which the favorite recipes are printed will be stuck together with dough-a sure sign of success.

Chapter 35

The Vocabulary

Mrs. A's ability to adjust to the words necessary for a particular article or occasion expanded with each new experience.

The fashion world was a continuous revolving door of words. Evening clothes were spectacular, sports clothes were clean-cut, and lingerie was fragile as a pink cloud while an unusual experience dress was precious. With each season, the fashion vocabulary evolved. One season it was the gentle tempo. Then there was the dress that flowed with the figure. One season the word for all fashion seemed to be functional. There were functional shoes, functional dresses and functional purses. The functional season was followed by luminous brilliance, soft-spoken grace and silken luxury.

Mrs. A fully understood her role in writing fashion copy. She appreciated that the busy housewife would sit down after the dinner dishes were done and the children were in bed and read about the early spring fashions which were being described as slender as a wand. She saw herself walking gracefully into a room where every person's head turned much like the scene from: "My Fair Lady" when Eliza Doolittle entered the room of upper class people. It's a dream like that of her husband who saw himself being driven to his office in a limousine.

When Mrs. A began writing a beauty column, she recognized that the woman wanted to be considered the pursued not the person doing the pursuing. The column was very successful. A survey revealed that the column was read equally by teenagers, career girls, young mothers, the over forty and those pushing sixty. It was discovered that men as well as women were reading the column.

The column encouraged people to write in with questions. One young man wrote that he was taking his girl to the high school prom. She didn't like pimples. He had pimples. What could he do to get rid of them?

There were so many questions that eventually a booklet "Lovely you" was developed with the answers. The sales of the booklet far surpassed all expectation. Again, Mrs. A had to learn a new vocabulary. She discovered that women loved the words such as fragrant, smooth, vivid and alluring but did not like seductive, dangerous and passionate.

The phrases "Beauty is something intangible "and "any woman can be lovely" were very much appreciated by most of Mrs. A's readers. A book on etiquette for the average family was developed when Mrs. A's research showed that no such book existed. It was a book for those people, who dined out now and then, attended a dinner party once in five years and who had a party in their own home once or twice a year.

For all such people, questions on the marriage of their daughter were of utmost importance. Mrs. A devoted forty pages in the etiquette book to questions that included who sat where during the wedding ceremony and in what order did people stand in the receiving line.

The formality of a funeral is important to help those who are mourning. The etiquette book attempted to deal with this very important crisis.

Most of the material that Mrs. A was writing about in these magazine articles and booklets was for the day in which she was living. Mrs. A always wanted to be relevant to her audience.

Because of her dedication to achieve giving aide to these people, suggestions made in the 30s, 40s and 50s were very significant for each decade. Because of her ability to adjust, she was very successful.

Chapter 36
Books

It was in the 1950s that Mrs. A began writing most of her books. These books were a diary of this amazing woman's life.

Kate Aitken's Ogilvie Cook Book was copyrighted in 1950. Never a Day So Bright was copyrighted in 1956. Travel Alone and Love It came out in 1958 followed by Making your Living is Fun in 1959. She had retired from radio in 1957.

Each of these books has been significant in the writing of this book. In fact, this book would not have been possible without her booksparticularly "Never a Day So Bright" and "Making Your Living is Fun". The detail in which Mrs. A wrote and her ability to tell a story are both important in the development of her own legacy. In her Ogilvie Cook Book the very first chapter of the book is called Daily Menu Building. The chapter begins with the statement "Vitamins have become a part of daily life, but not so many of us realize that, for health , vitamins and minerals should go hand in hand." Mrs. A, writing in the late 1940s, shows once again that she is the leader of the band. The vitamin movement was far from being in high gear in 1950 but Mrs. A was already seeing its significance. Later in the book she presents rules for good coffee making. There were no Tim Horton's or McDonalds. Periodically, this book has a "Note for Brides". There are specific helps for young developing cooks. There are helps for people hosting a large party such as how to make one hundred cups of tea.

Mrs. A published her first cook book in 1945, "Kate Aitken's Canadian Cook Book." This cookbook was updated and published in 1950, 1953, and 1964. There were annual reprints from 1965 to 1977. Its most recent reprint was in 2004. Mrs. A wrote and published a total of nine cook books. Through the years Kate published many pamphlets, articles and also booklets on cooking, including five titles in a series for Ogilvie Flour mills in 1934 to promote its Royal Household flours. Other publications were the monthly Good News Recipes brochures for Tamblyns and the Cooking Gossip bulletin for Canada Starch Ltd.; Kate tested all of her recipes at least three times. Most of this testing took place in her own kitchen with standard home equipment.

And of course, the recipes were all plain and straight forward.

The book ' Travel Alone and Love it' came at a time when middle class people were just beginning to travel to new ,more distant and exciting places. There were not books like this on the market. In today's world there are many people who have developed a book or books on how to travel based upon their own experience. Some of these experts have travelled in order to have a wealth of experience of tips for travelling. Mrs. A's travel had led her to learn firsthand what was necessary when travelling. She had not travelled for the purpose of developing tips on travelling. She had travelled because her job required her to. The tips that she shares in this book are tips that one might say were discovered in the school of hard knocks.

In Mrs. A's case, she was always a fast learner. She could even see a problem before it developed; As a result the reality was hard knocks were few and far between.

Chapter 37

Packing a Suitcase

In Mrs. A's early days of travelling about rural Ontario in the winter she quickly discovered that a hot water bottle was a necessity. The bed room temperature in many of the homes where she stayed was often frigid.

Mrs. A travelled so much that it was necessary for her to learn to pack what was necessary. Her luggage on plane travel had to be less than sixty-seven pounds. Her five trips around the world gave her experience to know exactly what she had to pack. A camera and a typewriter were necessary equipment. She wore a tweed suit and a matching cardigan on the plane. Her travel topcoat also served as an evening wrap. Her soft hats didn't crush. When she was attending an official event her clothes consisted of a navy suit and a contrasting hat. Her casual evening clothing was crease resistant. She had a short haired fur as an evening wrap. This fur was easy to pack.

Mrs. A understood the difference in custom from one country to the next and from one event to the next. Bare arms were not acceptable at government social affairs. The time for dinner to be served depended upon whether you were in Turkey, Australia or London.

To guarantee that she had the cosmetics that she wanted, she always packed enough for the entire trip.

The suitcase contained a small package of detergent, some bars of soap, a mending kit, a first aid kit, a tin of hard cookies, nylon lingerie, plenty of nylon stockings, always in the same shade and two pairs of shoes that were exactly alike in case a heal was broken.

In her book, Travel Alone and Like it, Mrs. A suggested the following for travel:

Leave your expensive furs and jewelry at home unless you expect to be formally entertained. Most people take too many clothes, too many shoes, indeed too much of everything. It's easy enough to pick up a cotton dress or an adorable wool sweater if you are running short.

The suit case should contain nylon under things, including two comfortable foundation garments, night clothes including one lightweight, easily packed dressing gown, plenty of stockings' in the same shade, two lightweight woolen suits with accessories of sweaters, scarves or pearls, two crease resistant cotton dresses when travelling to a warm country, a cardigan, a light weight topcoat, one short dinner dress with accessories, two pairs of matching shoes to be used for both daytime and evening wear, a soft hat, wash glove to match costumes, cosmetics, facial tissues, a medicine kit, containing aspirin and milk of magnesia tablets and two hand bags with one for daytime and one for evening.

The daytime bag should preferably be an over the shoulder bag which leaves both hands free. This bag should be carefully organized and should contain a letter from your bank, passports, visas, paper currency, a small cosmetic kit with folded tissue, a pen and pencil set, a notebook containing appointments, addresses and phone numbers, a small calendar, fold up scissors and a change purse.

CHAPTER 38

A Radio Script from 1956

This script of a broadcast on the CBC on September 10th, 1956 was aired less than a year before Mrs. A retired from her radio broadcast. In many ways, this broadcast and the accompanying letter summarize much of Mrs. A's life.

Box 549
Adelaide St. Post Office
Toronto, Ont.
Empire 4-2959

Kate Aitken
Broadcaster for Lipton Tea and Soups

Dr. S.R. McKelvey,
Beeton, Ontario.

Dear Doc:
Although I had planned on attending the re-opening of the church last Sunday visitors arrived just as I was leaving, which kept me tied to the spot.
However, we did do a broadcast about it drawing on our past memories, 6 copies of which are enclosed. We thought you might

*know of someone who would be interested in seeing it.
I hope the day was happy and successful.*

*Yours sincerely,
Kate Aitken*

KA; hk
Engl. 6.

Kate Aitken
Broadcaster for Good Luck Margarine

Trans Canada Net Work
Monday through Friday
11:30 AM
(Over C.F.R.B.) Toronto
11:30 AM

Monday, September 10th, 1956
Trans-Canada

Jingle : It's "Your Good Neighbour" time,
   Yes, it's Kate Aitken time,
   From here and there and everywhere,
   With news and views for you to share.
   So here's your daily date,
   When Lipton brings you Kate,
   Remember Lipton Shopping Day,
   And now here's Mrs. A.

Aitken: That's right — and hello Canada.

CY: Yes, here reporting to you for Lipton Soups, is "Your Good Neighbour — Kate Aitken." What's the billboard for today Mrs. A.?

Aitken : Now let me see. I think roughly we could divide it into three parts. A nostalgic bit that goes back to your childhood, with a gay, lilting tune that reminds you of the little church in which you were baptized – maybe married.

Horace: Music

Aitken: It's a modern bit, and one that's very much in our minds these days, when all Women's Organizations are starting a new year…"what happens to the retiring President?" What part should she play on the incoming executive? And then, of course, something not new and modern – something as old as time: "What are we going to eat today?" That's the ever present problem of every woman.

CY: Let's tackle the food first of all, because as you say Mrs. A., that's a daily labour of love.

Aitken: One thousand and ninety five meals ever year, and in this present year – Leap Year – it's one thousand and ninety eight, and you know as well as I that's where your Lipton Soups really give you a lift. Now we never serve them for breakfast…that's going a little too far…but we can use them for both lunch and dinner, and with great success. Monday – which is always a busy day – seems the ideal day for using the Lipton Beef Noodle Soup. And if you want to make a real meal of that hearty nourishing soup, do it this way – make up your Lipton Soup exactly according to directions, and while it's still simmering on the stove, drop in dumplings.

CY: Everybody loves them.
Aitken: Make up your own hot tea biscuit recipe, or use a tea biscuit mix, make them rather moist so that they'll drop off the spoon easily, rub the bowl of your mixing spoon with a little bit of margarine, which means the dumplings drop off magically – they don't stick – crowd them close together so that they ride on that soup

without sinking to the bottom. Put on a tight lid, and let the soup and dumplings cook to slow perfection for twenty minutes. Don't peek – don't lift – don't experiment Twenty minutes. Then spoon out that luscious Lipton Beef Noodle soup, complete with dumplings. It's a marvellous, satisfying luncheon or supper dish and one which leaves your family feeling happy and well satisfied. Easy to do...

CY: Delectable to eat...

Aitken: And full of nourishment. There's your quick meal for Monday washday.

Horace: Break

Aitken: And speaking of washday, here's a little tip for the sheets. Now all you experienced housewives know this – but sometimes the young brides haven't caught up with it. Don't fold your sheets centrewise over the clothes line, because that gives you a wear mark right down the centre of the sheet. Pin them by the hems, pulling them really straight, and you've given your sheets months more of wear.

Horace: Music

CY: Now into our women's organizations.

Aitken: Here's a figure I like to repeat. Of the approximately 16 millions of people in Canada – four million women belong to service organizations. They're all back full tilt into their fall season. In most women's organizations, the Presidential term is limited to two years. This year, a new president steps in, and the retiring president is more or less on the shelf. What does she do? How does she adjust herself to this new regime?

CY: Well, what does she do?

Aitken: If she's smart she forgets the past presidential years and becomes merely a member in ordinary standing. Never interfere with the new president – never hang on to what we might call "past glory", but the retiring president, if she's tactful and careful, can become a sort of elder statesman – giving her advice when it's asked for – keeping quiet when her advice isn't sought. But always being a tactful person who never imposes her past office on this new executive. It's quite a problem, but if, as so many presidents have, she has worked with that organization for years, then her interest is in the welfare of the group and not in her own personal pride. It's a new life, but it can be extremely satisfying. It means that the new executive will say, when a touchy problem comes up: "Let's ask Mrs. Smith – she knows all the answers."

CY: Now the nostalgic bit.

Aitken: Sunday, our church in the small village in which we were born, had a reopening, the church having been redecorated through the summer. To those of us in our family, it was quite a historic occasion, since the whole seven of us were baptized in that church, and in that same church we partook of our first sacrament. For those of you in the west and in the Maritimes, an Ontario village is not too well known, nor would you recognize the name of our small village, but it has quite a history. The first small settlement, 12 miles remote from a rail centre, was called Clarksville because of the family of Clarks who originally settled there. Then came a great change. The Postmaster, who was by way of being a small-town E.P. Talor – decided to go into the honey business, much to the disgruntlement of the farmers round about. He seeded vacant lots and roadways with sweet clover, to nourish his bees. The first run of honey from our locality to the Crystal Palace in London, and carried off all the red ribbons. British landed gentry, entranced with this Canada...

CY: And I gather from this that D.A. Jones was a great talker...

Aitken: He was indeed, and talked of Canada as if it were a land flowing with honey (let's forget the Milk.) So local gentry in England thought: "What an opportunity for the younger sons," and so all at once, as it were, the village became the centre of a honey-cult. So famous did it become, in its own small way, that the name was changed to Beeton – in deference to the bees. That was long before our time, but it's one of the legends of the village. Three churches were built there – the Anglican, the Presbyterian almost side by side with it, and the Methodist Church down Centre street. And it was this same D.A. Jones who planted Centre Street from one end to the other with an Avenue of Red Maples, so that in the early summer it was a deep, cool canyon – in the autumn it was a blaze of yellow and scarlet. Our church services were held in the afternoon, since our Minister had three appointments, morning, afternoon and evening, and for our family, Sunday was quite a day – indeed it started Saturday night when we were all thoroughly scrubbed – my mother ducking us one after the other into this huge tub of hot water. Everyone's hair was washed – the boys had to brush theirs, but mine was braided in tight braids, so that by Sunday, when it was brushed out, I looked exactly like a Fiji Islander. After the bath, we had to shine our shoes and lay out our Sunday clothes.

CY: But tell us about Sunday morning.

Aitken: Ah – Sunday morning. My father had one of the general stores in the village, and Saturday night was a late night. Farmers and their families coming in to shop, stayed until midnight, so we all slept in Sunday morning, but we were always wakened by the sound of my Father playing the old psalms of the church on the organ down in the parlour. Sunday morning was fun, and since we had to go to Sunday School at one thirty and stay right through for church, Mother gave us a hand-out lunch about twelve. Thinking back to yesterday – two of the things I remember most vividly are these. We had a black water spaniel – Cooney was his name and we really loved him, and Cooney hated to be left in the house alone for three hours, so he went to Sunday School with us and stayed through for the church service. Father thought this wasn't quite too decent, so he insisted on Cooney being tied up before Sunday School started. The first bell for Sunday School rang at one fifteen – that was signal for one of us to go, untie Cooney, who then ambled up to the church folded himself up as inconspicuously as possible in our pew, and stayed for the whole service.

CY: And the Anniversary services?

Aitken: Ah - there was something really special. Anniversary Sunday, which always came on the 24th May – was celebrated with two services, morning and evening. Old friends, neighbours, came for the whole day, visited with their relatives, and the morning services was just a little like an Old Boys Reunion, but it's the night service which I think none of us will ever forget. Our church was lit with oil lamps – brass bowls – huge chimneys – giving out their soft yellow radiance. Always, when the congregation sang: "Unto the Hills", and that too was a ritual – suddenly those oil lamps bloomed into a golden glory that I think none of us will ever forget.

Horace: Music

Aitken: In these modern days, when entertainment is so diverse and all-encompassing we sometimes forget that Canadians, in their earlier lives, found their social centre, their neighbourly companionship in the Church which they attended.

Horace: Music

CY: Well, which one of my favourite Lipton Soups are we going to talk about today, Mrs. A.? You make them all sound so good, I can never really make up my mind which one I like best!

Aitken: Well, the reason they sound good, Cy, is because they

ARE good! Every one of those home-made style Lipton Soups is a real meal-maker. That delicious Chicken Noodle for instance. Why, if I have a hurry-up meal, or leftovers to finish – I just start my family off with big, steaming bowls of Chicken Noodle – And my dinner's a success right away!

CY: Everyone loves that rich-tasting, goldeny chicken broth, flecked with nourishing egg noodles! And the reason it's so specially good – is because Lipton Chicken Noodle Soup tastes fresh home-made. Yes, you cook it yourself – just in a matter of minutes! All you do is add the contents of a package of Chicken Noodle to boiling water – let it bubble while you set the table – and there you have real, deep flavoured chicken noodle soup, with a flavour you just can't get any other way!

Aitken: The same thing goes for hearty Beef Noodle – tasty Tomato Vegetable – and that wonderful man-favourite...Lipton Onion Soup.

CY: There do sound good, Mrs. A., and I'm sure the ladies will appreciate the economy angle with Lipton Soups, too – they really are easy on the budget, aren't they? And of course, those neat little envelopes are so easy to carry home – so convenient to store!

Aitken: That's true Cy! I know I wouldn't be without them – and I'd always keep lots of Lipton Soups on my pantry shelf.

CY: Look for new deluxe blend Good Luck at your favourite store...you'll pick it out right away in that gleaming gold foil wrap! Yes, new deluxe blend Good Luck is now sealed in golden foil for complete flavour protection. And what flavour!

Aitken: New deluxe blend Good Luck is made from finer, costlier ingredients!

CY: It has a sweet, fresh delicate flavour...in fact, it tastes so good you have to be told it's margarine! Next time you shop...be sure to get lots of new deluxe blend Good Luck Margarine.

Horace: Music

CY: That's all the time we have, Mrs. A.

Aitken: Good day and Good luck.

CY: Kate Aitken has reported to you for Lipton Soups. Listen to Kate Aitken every day, Monday to Friday.

Horace: Music

CY: This is the Trans Canada network of the C.B.C

Chapter 39

The Spa

The spa is very much a part of Western Culture. The Greeks had many examples of spas. The Romans brought the spa to England. In the last century spas have become quite common in Western Europe. Although the health spa has not become a large feature in Canada, it appears to be growing slowly in popularity.

It is not surprising that Mrs. A would open one of the earliest Canadian spas in a large city area.

Mrs. A's Spa was west of Toronto in a quiet wooded area. It opened in 1953.

Mrs. A had been through the continuous experience of trying to get an appointment at a beauty salon on a Saturday when many of the shops in that day and age were closed. She discovered that many other women faced the same dilemma. And so, why not a weekend salon where hairdo's and pedicures would be part of a relaxing couple of days as beauty care was provided.

In preparation for the Spa opening Mrs. A actually worked in some salons in order to appreciate their operation. She came to realize that diet was an important part of such a venture in order to help those who wanted to lose a few pounds and those who wanted to add a few curves. Typically, she experimented with various diets in her own kitchen, with her family as the main participants.

A diet was developed that was low-calorie, took off weight and left the participant in a good mood, as there were no hunger pangs.

A lodge was built to host twelve guests at a time in single bedrooms with an adequate dining room and kitchen, a comfortable lounge for staff and room for the various beauty treatments.

The staff was carefully selected. Typical of Mrs. A; this venture was not developed to make money but to provide a service. The following is Mrs. A's description of a weekend at the spa.

We opened in late September, the ideal time.

The guests, checking in at four o'clock Friday afternoon eyed one another warily, as women always do when meeting strangers of their own sex. You could see them mentally tabulating one another's cars, mink coats and luggage. We knew the arrival of everyone at the same time would make rather a strained half-hour, so we worked out the following technique.

Each single bedroom had been named after one of the internationally known spas. On the outside of the doors were hand painted plaques with such names as Reykjavik, Iceland; Bath, England; and Hot Springs. There was also a picture of each spa. Inside, the bedrooms were done in pastel shades-pink, yellow, soft green, ivory, orchid and grey.

Our smart young hostess, checking in the guests, would say, "Ah, I think, we'll give you Wiesbaden. It exactly suits your personality. Michael will show you to your room." Intent on seeing how her personality had been transformed into lathe, plaster, paint and hangings, the guest sped on her way.

In each bedroom closet were placed the white terry-cloth robe, the soft slippers, the cosmetic bag, and the exercise outfit used by the guests. Directly the unpacking was done and the robe and slippers donned, each guest reported to the doctor for a thorough medical check-up. The reaction was amazing. Women, who for years had dreaded going to a doctor lest the ache here or the pain there was really serious, came out from that check-up smiling and relaxed.

Now they had something in common. Over a cup of tea in the lounge, one would say to another, "My dear, he says I'm as healthy as a horse. All I need to do is cut down on my starches." The underweight type would exclaim. *"Fancy me drinking a quart of whole milk every day! But that's what the doctor advises."* You could see the baker calling less frequently and the milkman with a steady order.

After the medical, the shampoos began; for our hair specialist maintained that hair could be more perfectly dressed if there was an interval of a few hours after the shampoo. Then came a deep massage, followed my complete cleansing of the face, neck, hands and arms.

As they waited for dinner a non-fattening cocktail was served. While sipping they learned one another's names, where they lived, the husbands' professions, how many children-all that sort of things.

The Friday-night dinner was more like a college reunion than anything else. Since all were going back for further treatment after dinner, they ate all in their white robes, hair tied up in bandanas. It was quite a contrast to see a formal, candlelit dinner-table surrounded by what seemed a group of happy, chattering girls in strict informal clothing. Since they all looked alike there was no need to keep up on any pretense; the barriers were down.

Before going to bed the hair was well brushed, the face cleansed and the finger-nails oiled. Ten o'clock was bedtime. From room to room the two Finnish masseuses would go to give the final back-rub. Saturday morning when the breakfast trays were served, the remark most commonly heard was, "I slept like a baby. Do you know, I haven't had a sleep like that for years?"

The Saturday routine included exercise, a walk in the woods, massage, Scotch hose treatment, manicure, pedicure, facial, and dressing of the hair. To the Saturday-night dinner husbands and sweethearts were invited. By the time they arrived these fresh skinned, immaculate beauties were radiant in evening gowns. When the arriving husbands looked round this bevy of attractive women, each would explain, "Now which one of you is my wife?"

There was no difficulty with the dinner-table conversation-it sparkled and flowed. When our men guests left at 11PM it took another hour of face-cleaning and back-rubbing to get everyone in the mood for sleep.

On Sunday, breakfast, again in bed, was an hour later. We had checked to find which church each guest wished to attend. It must be conceded that the guests from "The Spa" rated almost as much attention from the congregation as did the minister.

After Sunday dinner we had a class make-up. Seated in front of individual mirrors with the cosmetics selected by our beauty expert, each woman put into practice the things she had learned. By now they were completely unselfconscious and applied the make-up with all the care and exactitude that an artist gives a masterpiece. Such remarks would be passed as "I never knew before how to make my nose look smaller." Or "That deepened line on my lower lip certainly looks good doesn't it?"

The weekend concluded with high tea served at five o'clock, to which again the men and guests were invited. At these tea-parties there was always some new gimmick introduced. The guests would put on a fashion show, or demonstrate their exercises, or-most amusing of all-exchange hats and do a millinery exhibit.

When they said goodbye, not only had the guests themselves struck up lasting friendships but we had made new friends. To me it was most gratifying when guest after guest would say, "I feel ten years younger," or "You know when I came on Friday, I was right at the end of my tether. But now I feel as if I can face anything." To these busy women, these forty-eight hours was like an ocean voyage. They were babied, pampered and completely cut off from their normal heavy responsibilities. No meals to get, no dishes to wash, no phones to answer, no children to discipline, no decisions to make. The letting down of tension meant almost as much to them as the newly styled hair, or the flattering make-up.

Who were the guests? Business women, professional women, club presidents, private secretaries, brides-to-be and their mothers, librarians, and teachers. One thoughtful husband, in a family where there were four young children, sent his wife once a month to give her a break from the routine.

Was it an expensive project to set up? Indeed it was. The building had to be spacious and beautiful. In order to give the proper setting the grounds had to be landscaped and maintained. The equipment was costly. China, silver, crystal, linen and food all had to be of the best. A double supply of blankets, sheets, pillow cases, towels must be always kept on hand.

Was this establishment costly to maintain? A staff of twelve was necessary, one for each guest. Since every member of the staff was an expert, salaries were high. But it was one of the most rewarding and diverting enterprises on which we embarked. We all loved it. When the last car had driven away, we sat down and recapitulated the whole weekend. There was never any griping from the staff, nor did we at anytime have an unpleasant client.

But there was one weekend that topped all others. At this time I was doing a great deal of work amongst old age pensioners. In a moment of exuberance I suggested that we should set aside an early summer weekend for twelve senior citizens. The selection was left to the various welfare organizations.

We picked them up Friday afternoon-the youngest seventy-one, the oldest eight-two. They got the full treatment, even to make-up.

But it was the Saturday-night dinner that entranced us. The boy friends were of similar ages, but gallant as young beaus. After dinner when we went to the lounge I said, "Now what would you like to do?" Said a white haired, fragile little lady, "Let's turn on TV and look at the wrestling matches. They're always so exciting on Saturday night."

Chapter 40
The Retiring Years

Max Ferguson, who had begun his radio program during Mrs. A's greatest radio years, would periodically parody her on his Rawhide program. Max said that she was a Canadian institution just like the House of Commons and Air Canada.

Kate Aitken continued to be a spokesperson for women as well as a model for them.

It was in 1951 at an international meeting of women broadcasters that she stated that women had to accept greater responsibility because their influences and power were continuing to grow. The world could no longer be considered a man's world but was especially both a man's and women's world.

She now had her office in her home at SunnyBank where she continued to have a secretary. She would work at her writing and answer her continuous fan mail.

Her husband Henry retired from his work in Northern Ontario in 1958. He enjoyed the next three years at SunnyBank with Kate before his death in 1961 resulting from his arthritis.

After a morning of work in her office, Kate usually prepared lunch for those who were at the house. Her secretary and Henry shared lunch along with any of her daughter Mary's and her husband Bob's family who happened to be there. Mary ran a nursery school on the property. She and Bob had five grown children. One of Mary's sons, Scott, remembers often delivering the daily paper to his Grandmother.

Mrs. A was working in the family environment that she loved so much. Her other daughter Anne was not far away. Although she and her husband Clint moved around in the educational field, during much of these latter days of Mrs. A's life they spent much of the time in London with their four children. They were regular visitors to SunnyBank.

Mrs. A wrote articles in which she gave advice as to how a woman could raise a family and also have a career. She had the living example of both of her daughters.

In 1959 she was appointed to the CBC board of directors and served in that capacity for three years. During this time she also served as the CBC representative to UNESCO. During her years on radio she had covered UNESCO meetings in Geneva and New Delhi. Later in the 60s, Mrs. A served as the chair of Ontario UNICEF.

This grandmother found time to do some volunteer work with the South Peel Hospital. One can rightfully state in Mrs. A's life that once a community person, always a community person.

A fall on ice led to a broken hip. She recovered only to break a hip a second and third time. Mrs. A's granddaughter, Anne, remembers going to the hospital numerous times to visit her Grandmother with her Mother, Mary.

Mrs. A recovered from the second fall but did not recover from the third. She passed away at eighty one years of age. After a service at the Presbyterian Church in Streetsville, she was buried in the Aitken family plot in Beeton ,where her husband Henry had been buried a decade earlier.

Chapter 41

The Celebration

In June of 1973, a Memorial Day was held in the Beeton Park which is next door to the property that Kate and Henry had developed. Over a thousand people were in attendance that day as a memorial plaque was unveiled by her daughters Mary Hortop and Anne Thompson. Before they unveiled the plaque, Anne began her brief speech by saying thanks to everyone for the loving tribute being paid to her Mother. She concluded her words by saying that she and Mary always did things together and that Mary would conclude the thank you speech.

The Honorable Earl Rowe, who represented the Beeton area as the MP for over three decades had spoken earlier. He described Mrs. A as someone for whom his admiration grew and grew. He said she was unique, that she had boundless energy and imagination and she possessed a great desire to learn. She took women's liberation for granted as she developed her own opportunities into success stories.

The Women's Institute played a major role in the ceremony as three of its leaders addressed the crowd of friends, acquaintances and admirers. The Institute was also responsible for the lunch which was served following the unveiling.

One of the other speakers was the long time MPP for the area, Reverend A.W. Downer. He summed up the long public life of Mrs. A by stating that Kate Aitken had the gift to go to a location and describe it for her listeners so that it just lived.

Postscript

The year is now 2013 Mrs. A has been gone for over forty years —But what a legacy she has left.

The Canadian National Exhibition in 2013 officially opened inside of the Princess Gate. It was followed by a reception for invited guests. This was the first of many similar receptions during the Ex catered by employees of the Ex. It is over eighty years ago that similar receptions were began and catered to by Mrs. A and her staff.

Each day of the Ex included at least one cooking school World famous chefs were often the person in charge. It is ninety years ago that Mrs. A began her cooking schools on a stage under very primitive conditions.

As one travels about the Ex, a number of radio stations are part of the atmosphere. These stations make daily broadcasts, from the CNE grounds to their listening audience. Again, it is over eighty years ago that Mrs. A began the daily ritual of broadcasts live from the Exhibition to her eager listening audience.

An hour north of the Exhibition grounds one can visit the village of Beeton. Beeton was always home to Mrs. A. It is where she was born. It is where she is buried. Family members make sure that the grave plot is well maintained. The community park has the plaque honoring Mrs. A. It is found just inside the main gate. In the background of the memorial plaque is the agricultural building where Mrs. A's Mother won many red ribbons for her cooking and her crafts. The Beeton Fall Fair is now over one hundred and fifty years old. It is still going strong.

When a visitor walks the main street of the village, the structure of the former town hall still is a dominant part of the downtown area. Further to the west on the main street is St. Andrew, Presbyterian Church. It too, is a dominant piece of architecture where local people still hold regular worship services. Mrs. A grew up attending this church.

Many middle age women love to tell their story of how they came to receive their Kate Aitken cook book. The book was given by their grandmothers or mothers. In some cases, the cookbook was given as a special present to commemorate an important birthday or as a part of the wedding gift. These women not only know where these cook books are, these middle aged women still regularly use recipes which were a product of Mrs. A's kitchen.

Mrs. A's nine grandchildren are now, of the vintage age of grandparents themselves. Four of the grandchildren became teachers, one is a retired judge, and another has a high ranking position in the Anglican Church of Canada, a doctor and two others whom have been active in the business world. It sounds very much like the Robert Scott family. The Scriptures' state 'that by their fruit you shall know them'. It has also been said 'that the fruit will fall close to the vine".

A number of the great grandchildren have been involved in careers that require them to work and travel in other parts of the world away from their North American homeland.

Yes, Mrs. A,- thank you!!!!!!!

Kate's father, Robert Scott, in uniform

Kate, age 5, with brother Walter

Kate in Cypress Hill, Alberta

HERE'S MRS. A.

James Aitken (father of Henry) in front of Beeton Town Hall

Husband, Henry

The Mill in Beeton

Kate with one of her prize hens

HERE'S MRS. A.

Kate travelling about Ontario for the Department of Agriculture in the 1920s

Kate Aitken – CNE 1926 Canning Exhibition

Kate Aitken at the Chicago Women's Fair, 1927

Kate with Eleanor Roosevelt (the wife of American President Franklin D. Roosevelt)

Here's Mrs. A.

During World War II

Kate in her kitchen

Ron Pegg

Kate on her world travels

Kate with Gordon Sinclair

HERE'S MRS. A.

Kate with good friend Dr. S.R. McKelvey

Kate with D.W. Watson, Beeton's grand old man

Ron Pegg

Kate with grandchildren

Appendix

Mrs. A's Broadcast on the Opening of the Beeton Arena in 1948

Your Tamblyn Broadcast
With Kate Aitken – Monday through Friday 7:45pm (over CFRB)
225 Jarvis Street, Toronto

December 31, 1948.

Dr. S.R. McKelvey,
Beeton, Ontario.

Dear Doc:

Thanks so much for the notice you sent me regarding the opening of the Memorial Recreational Centre. I am sorry I couldn't get up for the dinner but I'm sure it was thoroughly enjoyed by all.
We are sending along a copy of the script from the Tuesday night broadcast when we did the story on Beeton. Thought you might enjoy reading it.

Yours sincerely,
Kate Aitken
KA:gl
Enc.

Ford Car. John Devereau Georgetown Ont.
Tamblyn Broadcast, Tuesday, December 28, 1948

Mrs. Aitken – Hello everyone. Big news tonight. It's another community recreation centre. Where? The famous town of Beeton in Simcoe County.......Better get on and open this rink.

Doc Lindsay – It's out at Beeton, 48 miles out Yonge Street. Now I think that's all I'm going to be allowed to say. Because our Mrs. A was born out there and when she gets bragging about the home town –

Mrs. Aitken – Who doesn't want to brag about his home town? To all of you listening to this broadcast who were born in or about the lovely little town of Beeton, what do you remember? Do you remember Centre Street, shady like a green canyon in the summer and like an avenue of glory in the fall when the leaves of the maple trees were scarlet and gold. It was the first settlers in this little town who planted that avenue of trees. They were spurred on by D.A. Jones, the man who established bee keeping in the small village and hence gave it its name – Beeton. Perhaps you will remember the Hills – perhaps, like us, you went sleigh riding there in the winter. Learned the joy of swooping down hill after hill until you came right to Main Street again. Or perhaps you went skating on the little rink behind the town hall. Do you remember the carnivals? Do you remember the little stove where we changed into skates and went clattering down to the ice? Do you remember the nights we had the band and the thrill of skimming around to music? If you do, then you'll be double glad to know that tonight the Memorial Rink of Beeton opens with a fast wild game of hockey between the Barrie Flyers and St. Mikes. Tomorrow that new memorial recreation centre will be officially opened and will make its bow to the whole community round about. Doc McKelvey – you see Doc, there's another one besides you –

Horace – Is he as good looking as Doc Lindsay?

Mrs. Aitken – Well, pretty nearly. Almost. Doc McKelvy has been one of the motivating spirits behind this whole recreation centre. The old town hall was sold; the recreation centre with the rink below and the community hall above was built back of the town hall. Tonight is going to be a gala night for Beeton and the whole community, And if happy ghosts walk, here are some of the valiant spirits who should be looking on as friend meets friend and neighbour greets neighbour tonight at Beeton. How many of you remember Mr. Joseph McPherson, famous school master who taught and trained hundreds of young Beetonians? Do you remember D.A. Jones, his beautiful gardens, his choice flowers, his strawberries and his really flowing profanity when things went against him? Do you remember the Bantings who lived just out from Beeton and who brought into the world young Fred, who afterwards becam world famous? And straight down the eighth line and up the hill lived Sir William Osler who made Canada famous all over the world. The Hammell family, there were five of them. All living on crown grants of land. Jack Hammill, one of the sons, made the northland. And bankers? Business men will remember G.T. Somers and his private bank in Beeton. Grownup school boys who are now grey-headed will remember the terrific hockey battles when Adgala Township came down and battled with the Beeton boys. Yes sir, I shouldn't be surprised too if the spirit of Joseph Wright, town clerk of this little municipality for so many years wouldn't be looking on tonight too. Home towns? There's nothing like them. Every old Beetonian tonight, I'm sure, is wishing this big project every success in the world – and saying – Go to it, boys. You'll soon have it paid for.

Horace – Skaters Waltz

Doc – Tell me, Mrs. A, before we leave Beeton, is there a Tamblyn store there?

Mrs. Aitken – No, there isn't. But there's the next best thing. Mr. Fachnie, who owns the local drug store, is a Tamblyn trained man.

Some Recipes from Kate's Canadian Cookbook

PLAIN PASTRY

3¼ cups sifted pastry flour 1 cup shortening
1 teaspoon salt Cold water (⅛ to scant ½ cup)

Sift the flour before measuring, then re-sift with the salt. Cut in the shortening with a dough blender, a cookie cutter or a case knife; it should be about as large as a pea. Sprinkle with just enough cold water to hold together. Mix lightly with a knife. Turn on a floured board and shape in a roll. Wrap in wax paper; chill slightly before rolling. This quantity will make a 2-crust pie, a 9″ baked shell, and ½ dozen tarts. The pastry need not all be baked at one time if the roll is kept chilled and tightly wrapped.

NOTE TO BRIDES: *It saves time and kitchen muss if enough pastry is made up for more than one pie. However, if you wish to make one single or double crust pie, here are the quantities:*

Quantities for One-Crust 9″ Pie

1 cup sifted pastry flour ⅛ cup shortening
⅛ teaspoon salt 2-2½ tablespoons cold water

Quantities for Two-Crust 9″ Pie

1¾ cups sifted pastry flour ½ cup plus 1 tablespoon
½ teaspoon salt shortening
4 tablespoons cold water

CHEESE PASTRY

3¼ cups sifted pastry flour ¾ cup cheese, grated
1 teaspoon salt Cold water (⅛ to ½ cup)
⅔ cup shortening

Sift the flour before measuring; sift again with the salt. Cut in the shortening, having the pieces fairly coarse; add the grated cheese; blend. Sprinkle with just enough cold water to bind the mixture. Mix lightly; wrap in waxed paper and chill before rolling. Yield: 2 covered 8″ pies.

NOTE TO BRIDES: *This pastry is especially good for apple pie, for meat pies and meat roll-ups.*

CORNFLAKES PIE CRUST

4 cups cornflakes, unrolled ¼ cup fine white sugar
⅛ cup melted butter

Roll the cornflakes till very fine; measure; there should be 1 cup. Mix with the melted butter, slightly warm, and the sugar. Brush a 9″ pie pan lightly with melted shortening. Line the bottom and sides with the cornflakes mixture; chill at least one hour before filling. Yield: One 9″ pie shell.

PASTRY

GINGERSNAP PIE CRUST

¼ cup brown sugar
⅓ cup softened butter
1½ cups gingersnap crumbs

Blend the brown sugar and softened butter until creamy. Add the crumbs and blend well. Rub a 9″ pie pan with oil; pat the crumb mixture firmly on the bottom and sides of the pan, crimping the edge with the tines of a fork; chill well before filling. This pie shell requires no baking and may be made the night before using. Yield: One 9″ pie shell.

APPLESAUCE PIE

Temperature: 425°F.
             350°F.
Time: 5 minutes
      40 minutes

Plain pastry
1 cup strained, thick, unsweetened applesauce
¾ cup white sugar
½ cup 18% cream
2 tablepoons melted shortening
2 eggs, beaten lightly
½ teaspoon grated nutmeg
2 teaspoons grated lemon rind
3 tablespoons lemon juice

Line a 9″ pie pan with pastry. Flute on an edge; bake in a hot oven (425°F.) for 5 minutes. Remove from the oven and fill with the following mixture:

Mix together the applesauce, sugar, cream, melted shortening, eggs, nutmeg, lemon rind and juice. Beat till well blended. Pour into the partially baked shell. Return to the oven (now 350°F.); continue baking until set. Serve slightly warm. Serves 6.

FRESH BLUEBERRY PIE

Temperature: 450°F.
             350°F.
Time: 15 minutes
      25 minutes

Plain pastry
4 cups fresh blueberries
2 tablespoons flour
½ cup white sugar
⅛ teaspoon salt
1 teaspoon lemon juice
1 tablespoon butter

Line a 9″ pie pan with plain pastry. Mix together the flour, sugar and salt. Sprinkle ¼ of this mixture on the uncooked bottom crust; add the blueberries; add the remainder of the sugar mixture; sprinkle with lemon juice; dot with butter. Flute on the top crust. Bake in a hot oven, 450°F. for 15 minutes; reduce the heat to 350°F.; continue baking until the berries are tender. Serves 6.

APPLE PIE

Temperature: 450°F. Time: 15 minutes
                350°F.   25-30 minutes

Plain pastry
2 tablespoons flour
1 cup white sugar
4½ cups apples, peeled, cored and sliced
1 teaspoon lemon juice
¼ teaspoon nutmeg
1 tablespoon butter

Line a 9" pie pan with pastry. Mix together the flour and sugar. Sprinkle half the mixture on the bottom crust. Add the apples, which have been peeled, cored and sliced ¼" thick. Sprinkle with lemon juice, the remaining sugar mixture and the nutmeg; dot with butter. Cover with the top crust; bake in a hot oven for 15 minutes; reduce the heat to 350°F. and continue baking until the apples are cooked. Serve slightly warm with cheese. Serves 6.

NOTE TO BRIDES: *When the green apples are available, core and slice but do not peel them; the green skin gives a typical flavor nothing else can touch.*

DUTCH APPLE PIE

Temperature: 450°F. Time: 20 minutes
                325°F.   20 minutes

Plain pastry
2 cups apples, cut in eighths
¾ cup brown sugar
¼ cup hot water
1 egg, well beaten
¾ cup cake or cookie crumbs
¼ cup sifted pastry flour
1 teaspoon cinnamon
¼ teaspoon nutmeg
⅛ teaspoon ginger
4 tablespoons softened fat

Line a 9" pie pan with plain pastry. Pare and core the apples; cut in lengths; arrange on the unbaked pastry in a regular pattern. Mix together the brown sugar and hot water; add the well beaten egg; pour the whole mixture over the apples. Mix together the crumbs, flour, spices and softened fat; sprinkle over the pie filling. Bake in a hot oven (450°F.) until the mixture begins to brown, about 20 minutes; reduce the heat to 325°F. and continue baking another 20 minutes. Serve slightly warm with cheese. Serves 6.

BUTTERSCOTCH CHIFFON PIE

Baked pie shell—9"
1 tablespoon gelatine
¼ cup cold water
3 eggs, separated
¾ cup brown sugar
1 cup hot milk
⅛ teaspoon salt
1 teaspoon butter
½ teaspoon vanilla
2 tablespoons white sugar

PASTRY

Soften the gelatine in the cold water for 5 minutes. Beat the egg yolks slightly; add the sugar, milk and salt. Blend well with the dover beater; cook over boiling water till the mixture coats the back of a spoon, stirring occasionally. When thick, remove from the heat; stir in the softened gelatine, butter and vanilla. Beat with a dover beater till creamy; fold in the stiffly beaten egg whites to which has been added the white sugar. Pour into the baked shell. Chill 1½ hours before serving. Serves 6.

BUTTERSCOTCH PIE

Baked pastry shell—9″
2 tablespoons fat
¾ cup brown sugar
1¾ cups hot milk
4 tablespoons corn starch
4 tablespoons cold milk
⅛ teaspoon salt
2 eggs, separated
1 teaspoon vanilla
3 tablespoons white sugar
1 teaspoon corn starch

Melt the fat in the top of the double boiler; blend in the brown sugar; let cook over direct heat till bubbly but not burned. Add the hot milk slowly; stir and cook till blended. Make a paste of the 4 tablespoons of corn starch, cold milk and salt; stir into the milk mixture; stir and cook till thick and smooth. Place over rapidly boiling water; cover and cook for 10 minutes stirring occasionally. Separate the eggs; beat the yolks slightly. Combine them with a little of the hot mixture; stir back into the filling. Blend well; continue cooking for 3 minutes. Remove from the heat; add the vanilla. Beat till smooth; pour into the baked shell. Beat the egg whites till stiff and glossy; add 3 tablespoons white sugar and 1 teaspoon corn starch; beat again till the mixture peaks. Pile lightly on the pie filling; brown in a 350°F. oven. Serves 6.

CANNED CHERRY PIE

Temperature: 425°F.
Plain pastry
½ cup white sugar
2 tablespoons flour
Dash of salt
Time: 40 minutes
¾ cup juice drained from cherries
2 cups canned cherries, drained
1 tablespoon butter
¼ teaspoon cinnamon

Line a 9″ pie pan with plain pastry. Mix together the sugar, flour and salt; sprinkle ¼ of the mixture on the bottom crust. Add the remainder to the cherry juice. Stir till smooth; cook over low heat until smooth and clear, about 5 minutes. Add the cherries, butter and cinnamon; pour into the lined pie plate. Cover with a top crust; bake in a hot oven till the crust is golden. Serves 6.

Some Recipes from Kate's Ogilvie Cookbook

USE OGILVIE ALL-PURPOSE FLOUR AND

COCOA CAKE
(One Egg)

Temperature: 375° F. Time: 30–35 minutes

- ¼ cup cocoa
- ¼ cup boiling water
- ⅓ cup shortening
- ¾ cup brown sugar
- 1 egg, well beaten
- 1¼ cups sifted pastry flour
- ⅛ teaspoon salt
- ¾ teaspoon baking soda
- ½ cup sour milk

Measure cocoa into mixing bowl; add boiling water; stir till d[is]solved. Cream together shortening and sugar; add well beaten eg[g] beat till fluffy. Combine with cocoa mixture and beat well. Add sift[ed] dry ingredients alternately with sour milk. Blend; pour into oiled p[an] 8" x 6" which has been lined with waxed paper; bake in modera[te] oven until done. This cake is very tender, so let stand in pan f[or] minutes before inverting to cool. Ice with plain Butter Icing. Yie[ld] 9 pieces.

CRUMB CAKE

Temperature: 375° F. Time: 35–40 minutes

- 2 cups sifted pastry flour
- 1 cup brown sugar
- ¾ cup shortening

Sift together flour and brown sugar; rub in shortening with tips [of] the fingers. When mixture is crumbly, take out ¾ cup; to remain[der] add all at once and without beating:

- ¼ teaspoon salt
- ¼ teaspoon nutmeg
- ¼ teaspoon cloves
- 1 teaspoon cinnamon
- 1 egg, unbeaten
- 1 cup raisins, chopped
- ¾ cup thick sour milk
- ¼ cup brown sugar
- 1 teaspoon baking soda

Beat this mixture until smooth; pour into oiled pan 8" x 1[2"]; sprinkle reserved crumb mixture over raw batter. Bake in moder[ate] oven until done. Yield: 20 pieces.

RED DEVIL'S FOOD CAKE

Temperature: 375 F. Time: 35–40 minutes

- ⅓ cup shortening
- 3 squares (3 oz.) unsweetened chocolate, grated
- 1¼ cups brown sugar
- ¾ cup water
- 2 eggs, unbeaten
- 1 teaspoon vanilla
- 1½ cups sifted cake flour
- ¾ teaspoon salt
- ¾ teaspoon baking soda
- ¾ teaspoon baking powder
- ⅜ cup thick sour milk

Melt shortening in top of double boiler; add grated chocolate; until melted. Add sugar and water; beat until well blended. Rem[ove]

46

OGILVIE OATS IN PREPARATION OF THESE RECIPES

from heat; cool to room temperature. Add eggs, one at a time; beat until light; add vanilla. Add sifted dry ingredients alternately with sour milk. Pour into oiled pan 8" x 8" lined with waxed paper; bake in moderate oven until done. Yield: 12–16 pieces.

CANADIAN FRUIT CAKE

Temperature: 300° F.   Time: 2 hours

1 cup diced salt pork
1 cup boiling water
2 teaspoons baking soda
1 cup dark molasses
1 cup brown sugar
2 eggs, separated
1 teaspoon cloves
2 teaspoons cinnamon
4 cups sifted all-purpose flour
1 cup raisins, chopped
1 cup mixed peel, chopped
1½ teaspoons lemon flavoring
1 teaspoon grated lemon rind

Dice pork very fine, taking out any bits of lean meat; cover with boiling water; let stand 5 minutes. Add baking soda, molasses and sugar; stir until well dissolved; add well beaten egg yolks. Add sifted dry ingredients alternately with chopped fruit. Add lemon flavoring and grated rind; fold in stiffly beaten egg whites. Pour into 2 square pans 8" x 8" x 3½" which have been lined with heavy brown paper and oiled; bake in slow oven. Store 2 weeks before using. Yield: 6 lbs. of cake.

CHRISTMAS CAKE (Dark)

Temperature: 275° F.   Time: 3 hours

1 cup butter
1¼ cups brown sugar, firmly packed
½ cup corn syrup
4 eggs, well beaten
¼ cup strawberry jam
¼ cup candied lemon peel, chopped
½ cup candied citron peel, chopped
½ cup candied cherries, chopped
¼ cup candied orange peel, chopped
1 cup seedless raisins, chopped
1 cup currants, washed, and dried
½ cup nuts, chopped
2½ cups sifted pastry flour
½ teaspoon baking soda
¼ teaspoon salt
½ teaspoon cinnamon
¼ teaspoon cloves
¼ teaspoon mace

Cream butter; gradually beat in sugar and corn syrup; add well beaten eggs. Add jam, peel, fruit and nuts. Gradually add sifted dry ingredients; mix well. Pour batter into oiled square pan 8" x 8" x 3½" which has been lined with heavy brown paper; bake in slow oven until firm and golden brown. To prevent cake drying out, cover with heavy brown paper, remove for last half hour of baking. Glaze cake or ice with Almond Icing. Yield: 4 lbs.

Kate Aitken Memorial Day Program

Kate Scott Aitken Memorial Day
June 3, 1973
Community Park – Beeton, Ontario

Chairman – Dr. S.R. McKelvey

O Canada

Welcome to Beeton..Reeve S.R. McKelvey
Welcome to Simcoe County...........................Warden James Wales
Simcoe County Historical Association..............Mr. David Phillips, Chairman of the Board Simcoe Country Women's Institute....................Mrs. Gordon Mallion
South Simcoe Women's Institute.........................Mrs. W. Trotter
Beeton Women's Institute..................................Mrs. Earl Stewart
Arthur E. Evans, M.L.A., Centre Simcoe
Rev. A.W. Downer, M.L.A., Dufferin-Simcoe
"Kate Scott Aitken, The citizen".........................Hon. W.E. Rowe
Unveiling of memorial plaque by daughters.......Mrs. Anne Thompson
Mrs. Mary Hortop
Dedication of plaque by Rev. Basil P. Das, Presbyterian Church, Beeton
Lunch in Memorial Hall, by Beeton Women's Institute

God save the Queen
All Welcome

2:00 PM Sunday June 3, 1973
Do hope you can come

Letters from the Memorial Celebration and Tribute; June 3, 1973

My dear Dr. McKelvey –

Thank you so very much for the invitation to Beeton on Sunday, June Third. As the widow of Bruce Scott, Kate's oldest brother, and the only survivor of that generation of husbands and wives in the Scott family, I feel it is a privilege to be with others of Kate's friends, relatives and associates who will be honoring her memory. As well as being a sister-in-law we were very good friends. My daughter, Anne Scott Duncan (Mrs. Gordon M.) of King City and my second son, Ronald, a Teacher in Sarnia, will also be present.

If we have not met at one of Kate's summer reunions, I hope to meet you at the memorial meeting.

Yours sincerely – Mary G.H. Scott
Mrs. R. Bruce Scott
35 DonegalDr.
Toronto 17. Ont

Ron Pegg

125 College South, Apt. 104,
Sarnia, Ontario N7T-2Z5
27 May, 1973

The Secretary,
Corp'u of the Village of Beeton,
Beeton, Ontario

Sir:

Please pass along to the Village Council my thanks for sending me an invitation for the Kate Scott Aitken Memorial Day, to be held in Beeton on 3 June, 1973.

May I also commend your action in organizing such a day for one whom I have always considered to be an (perhaps the) outstanding Canadian woman of her generation. I believe this to be so not only because she was successful in her various endeavours but because she also retained her feeling for others around, in particular her family (really, her 'clan') and those from the Beeton area with whom she had grown up, worked, and played. I realize that, as one of her 'family', I ought not to be extolling the greatness of my "Auntie Kate", but I really do not think I need to aplogise to you for doing so.

Unless circumstances intervene, I shall be among those present in Beeton on Sunday, 3 June next, in the community Park at the Ceremony of the unveiling of the historic plaque in memory of Kate Scott Aitken.

Thank you once again for your kind invitation.

Sincerely,
Ronald Scott.

1 Renfrew Avenue
Ottawa, Ontario
K1S 1Z2
May 24, 1973

Dr. S.R. McKelvey
Beeton
Ontario

My dear Dr. McKelvey:

I am grateful to someone for having sent me the announcement of the Kate Scott Aitken Memorial Day.

Though I am still surviving, I am at the 253rd day of trying to get a fractured hip in operation again. Consequently, I can only send my greetings and respectful memory of one of the brightest and gayest of my contemporaries.

It should be recorded that Kate Aitken built her national and international reputation on broadcasting which was wholesome, bright and humorous and fully served the cause which was always closest to her heart, the Women's Institutes and their motto "For God and Country".

Yours sincerely,
Charlotte Whitton
Former Mayor of Ottawa

American Mothers Committee, Inc.
Waldorf-Astoria Hotel
301 Park Avenue
New York, N.Y.
PL 5-2539 – PL 5-2755

May 30, 1973

Mrs. Dorothy Lewis
Chairman, Advisory Council
Honorary President

Dr. S.R. McKelvey
3719 Mississauga Road
R.R. #4, Mississauga, Ont.
Canada

Dear Dr. McKelvey

Thank you for the invitation to attend the Kate Scott Aitken Memorial Day, to be held on June 3rd at Beeton, Ontario. Mr. Lewis and I would be so happy to be present to honor a great lady. Unfortunately, we cannot leave New York at this time.

During the years that I was President of the International Ass'n of Women in Radio and Television, she was a distinguished member of this international organization. I saw her many time in New York on her frequent visits, and cherish one of her autographed cookbooks. I think we can truly say that during recent years she was the most successful and distinguished woman broadcaster/commentator in the world. Please extend to her family our congratulations on this brilliant occasion.

We appreciate the memorial booklet very much.
Sincerely,
(Mrs.) Dorothy Lewis

Personal address: 414 East 52nd Street -Apt.4-B
New York, N.Y. 10022

Reeve S.R. McKelvey
Beeton, Ontario

Dear Doc,

It is hard to express what is in our hearts except to say a great big "thank you" to you personally and to the Village of Beeton for the wonderful Memorial Day on Sunday for mother. To be honoured and remembered by your own people is perhaps the greatest tribute that can be paid to any person.

The service in the park was so appropriate in every detail and the warm and generous hospitality at the reception was so typical of Beeton.

We can only say "thank you one and all" and God bless Beeton.

Sincerely,

Mary Hortop and Anne Thompson

June 5, 1973

Thorndale, Ontario
July 27/72

Dear Dr. S.R. McKelvey
Reeve of Beeton
Beeton, Ontario

Dear sir;
Please excuse my tardiness in not writing sooner to thank you for taking time to show us around as well as the home of the late Mrs Kate Aitken when we were on our East Middlesex Institute Bus Trip.

It was most interesting and most enjoyable.

Again thanks
Mrs Kenneth Hogg
Thorndale

Bibliography

(1) News Worthy
The Lives of Media Women
By Susan Crean
Copyright 1985

Printed by Stoddart Publishing
A Division of General Publishing, Co. Ltd.
30 Lesmill Road
Toronto, Canada
M3B 2T6

(2) Kate Aitkens
Canadian Cookbook
First Published, Montreal: The Standard 1945
Copyright 2004 Estate of Kate Aitken
Whitecap Books Ltd.
351 Lynn Avenue
North Vancouver
British Columbia, Canada
V7J 2C4

(3) Kate Aitkens Ogilvie
Cookbook
Published by Wm. Collins & Co. Ltd
London, New York, Toronto
Copyright 1950 by Kate Aitken
(4) Never a Day So Bright
Published by Longmans, Green & Company
20 Cranfield Rd., Toronto 16
Copyright Canada 1956
By Kate Aitken

(5) Kate Aitken
Part of "The Canadians, a Continuing Series."
Published by Fitzhenry & Whiteside Ltd.
Don Mills, Ontario
1979, Jean Cochrane, Author

(6) Travel Alone and Love It
Longmans, Green & Co.
20 Cranfield Road,
Toronto 16
Copyrighted 1958
By Kate Aitken

(7) Making your living is fun
Longmans, Green & Co.
Toronto & New York
20 Cranfield Road,
Toronto 16
Copyrighted 1959
By Kate Aitken

(8) The Archives of the Canadian National Exhibition

(9) The Archives of the Museum on the Boyne, Alliston

(10) The Files of Dr. SR. McKelvey & Bert Platt

(11) Conversations with some of Mrs. A's grandchildren

(12) Quotes in the book by Mrs. A are either from "Never a Day So Bright" or "Making your living is fun" unless otherwise noted

OTHER BOOKS BY RON PEGG

Tribute
978-1-77069-585-6
"For God so loved the world that he gave his one and only Son, that whoever believes in him shall not perish but have eternal life," (John 3:16, NIV).

It was in the late 1970s when the Walls family and Frank Macintyre of the Dundalk Herald gave Ron Pegg the opportunity of writing a weekly column for the Flesherton Advance. During the next three decades he wrote the column under a number of different names. This book includes articles from that column, along with many recent works.

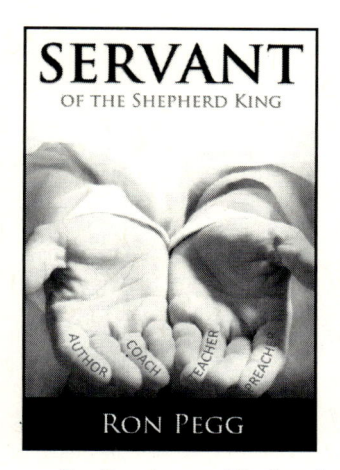

Servant of the Shepherd King
978-1-77069-557-3
Can one servant make a difference? Beginning in his early years during the Great Depression in Beeton, ON, this autobiography delves in to Ron Pegg's life story, chronicling the experiences that shaped him into the person he has become. He has taught school for 34 years, coached 213 teams in various sports over a 47-year coaching career and was the winning coach in over 2,400 games and 54 championship or finalist teams. He has belonged to various prayer groups as well as serving as a church elder and Sunday School superintendent for over 35 years. He has been lay supply preacher for 60 years. He is one of three life members of Ontario Baseball.

Ron Pegg
Box 213
Flesherton, ON N0C 1E0
(519) 924-3538
email: crpegg@bmts.com